W9-DHI-707

Angola, Mozambique, and the West

THE WASHINGTON PAPERS

. . . intended to meet the need for an authoritative, yet prompt, public appraisal of the major developments in world affairs.

Series Editors: Walter Laqueur; Amos A. Jordan

Associate Editors: William J. Taylor, Jr.; Thomas Bleha

Executive Editor: Jean C. Newsom

Managing Editor: Nancy B. Eddy

President, CSIS: Amos A. Jordan

MANUSCRIPT SUBMISSION

The Washington Papers and Praeger Publishers welcome inquiries concerning manuscript submissions. Please include with your inquiry a curriculum vitae, synopsis, table of contents, and estimated manuscript length. Manuscripts must be between 120–200 double-spaced typed pages. All submissions will be peer reviewed. Submissions to *The Washington Papers* should be sent to *The Washington Papers*; The Center for Strategic and International Studies; 1800 K Street NW; Suite 400; Washington, DC 20006. Book proposals should be sent to Praeger Publishers; One Madison Avenue; New York NY 10010.

The Washington Papers/130

Angola, Mozambique, and the West

Helen Kitchen, Editor

Published with The Center for
Strategic and International Studies
Washington, D.C.

New York
Westport, Connecticut
London

Library of Congress Cataloging-in-Publication Data

Angola, Mozambique, and the West.

(Washington papers, ISSN 0278-937X ; 130)
"Published with the Center for Strategic and
International Studies, Washington, D.C."
"Praeger special studies. Praeger scientific."
Includes index.
1. United States – Foreign relations – Angola.
2. United States – Foreign relations – Mozambique.
3. Angola – Foreign relations – United States.
4. Mozambique – Foreign relations – United States.
I. Kitchen, Helen A.   II. Georgetown University.
Center for Strategic and International Studies.
III. Series.
E183.8.A5A54 1987   327.73067'3   87-21818
ISBN 0-275-92879-9
ISBN 0-275-92880-2 (pbk.)

The *Washington Papers* are written under the auspices of The Center
for Strategic and International Studies (CSIS) and published
with CSIS by Praeger Publishers. The views expressed in these papers
are those of the authors and not necessarily those of the Center.

Library of Congress Catalog Card Number: 87-21818
ISBN: 0-275-92879-9 (hb)
        0-275-92880-2 (pb)

First published in 1987

Praeger Publishers, One Madison Avenue, New York, NY 10010
A division of Greenwood Press, Inc.

Printed in the United States of America

The paper used in this book complies with the Permanent
Paper Standard issued by the National Information Standards
Organization (Z39.48-1984).

10 9 8 7 6 5 4 3 2 1

Contents

II. Mozambique

Introduction

One of the least predictable developments of 1987 in the never-ending swordplay in the corridors of power in Washington has been the emergence of U.S. relations with a former Portuguese colony, Mozambique, as the single most controversial African policy issue. In an irony reminiscent of the debates over Angola during the Carter administration, the principal actors in the 1987 confrontation over Mozambique are all nominal supporters of President Reagan.

Defense of the existing policy of full recognition of and supportive economic ties with the FRELIMO government of President Joaquim Chissano is centered in the Department of State and extends to significant personalities within the revamped National Security Council, the Agency for International Development, and some elements (but by no means all) of the Department of Defense, and the CIA. Leading the attack against administration policy and for recognition of the Resistência Nacional Moçambicana (known as Renamo or the MNR) as "anti-Communist freedom fighters" worthy of U.S. recognition and support are several powerful Republican members of Congress (including Senators Jesse Helms and Robert Dole), backstopped by an accelerating media blitz from a range of political action groups, newspapers and journals, and other fora on the right of the political spectrum.

In the case of Angola, the policy community has been in disaccord for a dozen years over the still-unresolved issue of diplomatic recognition. Feelings also run strong on the stamp of approval given by Congress in 1985 to the principle of providing limited U.S. covert military assistance to the antigovernment forces of Jonas Savimbi's UNITA. In 1987, the dispute over Angola policy took on another dimension as pressure groups attacking administration Africa policy from the Right stepped up a campaign to eliminate the U.S. corporate presence (especially that of oil companies) from Angola. Calls are being voiced for a Defense Department boycott of all Chevron products and for imposition of a trade embargo against Angola aimed at curtailing that government's ability "to pay for Cuban troops and Soviet arms." The case for economic sanctions is flawed, in the view of corporate principals and apolitical analysts here and abroad, because of the virtual certainty that European oil interests are waiting in the wings to take over any abandoned U.S. operations. As in the case of Mozambique, the Angola sanctions campaign is led by individuals who view Africa primarily as a segment of the East-West chessboard.

The high ratio of heat to light in much that is being written and said about Mozambique and Angola in the United States in the 1980s renders especially timely the publication of this collection of cogent, nonpartisan assessments of the situation on the ground in the two countries and of U.S. policy options. The eight chapters were selected from 73 essays we have published over the past five years as issues of the *CSIS Africa Notes* "briefing papers for decision makers" series. Although the components were not originally envisaged as parts of a single book, each contribution has stood the test of time, and dovetails with the others into a cohesive whole.

One reason for the high credibility of these essays is the quality of the authors. Although they come from different professional and geographical bases – John Marcum from the United States, Gillian Gunn from Britain, and Winrich Kühne from West Germany – they share a unique knowledge of the recent history and key personalities of the two countries under review, a concern for accuracy of detail, an aversion to allowing stereotypes to pass unexplored, and the commitment of the CSIS African Studies Program to "unsimplifying" and "demystifying" African issues and choices.

While I believe that this collection will be especially helpful to contemporary U.S. policymakers and prospective electoral candidates seeking to separate realities from red herrings in southern Africa, it will also be of interest to European and African readers. Moreover, because each entry carries a dateline indicating that this was how a particular issue or situation was evolving at a given time, the book should remain a valuable reference source for many years.

Helen Kitchen
Director of African Studies
Center for Strategic and International Studies

July 1987

About the Authors

John A. Marcum is author of the classic two-volume work, *The Angolan Revolution — The Anatomy of an Explosion, 1950–1962* (MIT Press, 1969) and *Exile Politics and Guerrilla Warfare, 1962–1976* (MIT Press, 1978). His other major publications include *Education, Race, and Social Change in South Africa* (University of California Press, 1982). Dr. Marcum served as academic vice chancellor of the University of California at Santa Cruz from 1979 to 1984, is a former president of the 2,000-member African Studies Association, and frequently travels to southern Africa.

Winrich Kühne is head of the Africa department at the Research Institute for International Politics and Security of the Stiftung Wissenschaft und Politik in Ebenhausen near Munich. His articles on African affairs and on Soviet policy toward the Third World have appeared in a number of German as well as international journals, and he is the author of *Die Politik der Sowjetunion in Afrika* (1983) and *Südafrika und seine Nachbarn: Durchbruch zum Frieden?* (1985).

Gillian Gunn is a visiting fellow in the CSIS African Studies Program. From 1981 until she was named a Rockefeller Foundation international relations fellow in March

1984, she served as Africa editor of Business International, a London-based research, publishing, and consulting firm. As a specialist in Africa's economic development (her graduate studies were at the London School of Economics), she has written for the *International Herald Tribune* (Paris), *The Times* (London), *The Guardian*, *Africa Economic Digest*, and *African Business*. She devoted her two years as a Rockefeller Fellow to in-country studies of Mozambique's and Angola's relations with the West since independence.

I

Angola

1

UNITA: The Politics of Survival

John A. Marcum

February 1983

In early 1976, the remnants of an ill-trained peasant army retreated into the vast wilderness of southeast Angola. Its rivals, spearheaded by a Soviet-armed Cuban expeditionary force, drove the army's several thousand disheveled soldiers into the sanctuary of a sparsely peopled savannah from which they had earlier waged a protracted, small-scale guerrilla war against Portuguese colonial rule. There, most observers expected the army slowly to disintegrate. Over time, however, the world heard just often enough of ambush and sabotage by rusticated insurgents of the União Nacional para a Independência Total de Angola (UNITA) to know that they survived as a political and military force. In 1983, seven years after defeat in the 1975–1976 war, UNITA leaders and guerrillas not only survive as a reality to be reckoned with inside Angola. They have become a significant factor in the complicated quest for an internationally sanctioned political settlement in Namibia.

What is this UNITA that refused to die and instead continues to challenge the rule of its victorious rival, the Movimento Popular de Libertação de Angola (MPLA)? An anti-Communist "Cinderella" force for national liberation? A tribalist, racist movement whose Faustian leadership sold its soul to South Africa? To answer these and less

3

tendentious questions, it may help to look behind partisan debate to the origins, character, and history of UNITA.

The Savimbi Factor

In the eyes of many, UNITA is synonymous with its leader, Jonas Malheiro Savimbi. It is Savimbi's tenacity, Savimbi's ambition, Savimbi's nationalism that define the movement. However, opinion concerning his leadership differs widely. The editor of the Johannesburg *Sunday Times*, Tertius Myburgh, characterized the Savimbi he traveled to the Angola bush to interview in mid-1982 as a "gifted, brave, and unshakably dedicated man," a "sturdily independent spirit" on a "long march to the presidency of an Angola free of Cuban-Soviet domination." And if on that march he "can be assisted by pragmatic, but cautious, contact with South Africa, so be it." Tanzania's President Julius Nyerere, among other African political opinion leaders, perceives Savimbi as a political opportunist who betrayed Africa when he secretively aligned UNITA with South Africa.

Savimbi was born in 1934 at a railway village in Angola's central highlands where his father served as stationmaster. His parents, described by a United Church missionary as being of "exceedingly humble, primitive, pagan background," had been converted to Protestant Christianity in their youth. As a lay preacher, his father, Lote Savimbi, founded a series of small churches and schools along the Benguela railroad. Local Catholic priests repeatedly pressured colonial authorities to have Lote Savimbi transferred. The government complied, but each time it moved him, local supporters rallied to keep his church and school alive. "The end result was that all up and down the line there was a string of strong churches and elementary schools." (Missionary letter by John A. Reuling, March 2, 1959). This spirit of religious independence in the face of repressive authority had a formative impact on Jonas Savimbi. He — like other Angolan youngsters whose education began at

United Church, Methodist, and Baptist mission schools —
was influenced by those who preached and practiced an
imported social gospel. One result was a disproportionate
number of Protestants within the leadership ranks of Angolan nationalist movements that developed in the 1950s and
1960s.

After finishing Portuguese-run secondary school at
"the very top of his class," Jonas Savimbi is reported by
missionary sources to have confronted strong pressure to
join the local Catholic church in return for scholarship aid.
He refused. Reinforcing this portrayal of Savimbi as a person of principled independence from childhood on, UNITA
publicists have stressed his "stubbornness in the face of
injustice," citing how, even as a youth, he had the courage to
challenge "a team of Portuguese settlers" that was "twisting
the rules" during a village football match.

Savimbi continued to quarrel with Portuguese authority when, after the United Church sent him to Lisbon in
1958 to study medicine, the political police (PIDE) pressed
him to inform on other Angolan students. He refused and,
at the onset of 1961, shortly before anticolonial insurgency
broke out in Angola, fled to Switzerland. There, in June
1965, following an interlude of political activity in Africa,
he completed, not a medical degree as some reports would
have it, but a *licence* in political and legal sciences at the
University of Lausanne.

First as an associate of the Zaire (Congo)-based Bakongo leader, Holden Roberto (1961–1964), and then as
head of his own movement (1966 on), Savimbi entered the
realm of exile politics. Characterized by intrigue, self-delu-
sion, frustration, and factional conflict, exile politics re-
quires of its actors special gifts of guile, resilience, and luck.
Savimbi's survival attests to an uncommon endowment of
all three. Along the way, he has surmounted many setbacks.

Take, for example, the disaster of 1967, when he was
leading UNITA from an exile base in Zambia. In August of
that year, his guerrillas attacked and disrupted traffic on
Angola's Benguela railroad, which carried significant

amounts of Zaire's and landlocked Zambia's mineral exports to the sea and world markets. He assured Zambian authorities that he had sent orders to his men inside Angola not to cut the railroad, but that the orders had arrived too late. However, a combination of factors – pressure from the Portuguese government, pressure from Tanganyika Concessions Ltd. (which owned the railroad), exploitation of the situation by the rival MPLA, and suspicions that had been aroused by UNITA's cooperation with local opponents of Zambian President Kenneth Kaunda in carrying out organizational efforts among Angolan refugees – led the Zambian government to arrest and expel him. From a back alley headquarters in the Zambian capital, UNITA issued a rueful communiqué: "Dr. Jonas Savimbi has fallen victim of his hard work in Angola. . . . This does not mean that UNITA is dead. [His] absence . . . is a temporal setback to the party and the revolution as a whole, but the work he started will gain momentum and prosper against the wishes of Portuguese imperialists and their financiers. Dr. Jonas Savimbi's absence will be felt by all peace-loving people of the world."

His absence was indeed sorely felt by his followers. But UNITA did not die. A year later (1968), with the help of Namibian nationalists of the South West Africa People's Organization (SWAPO), Savimbi successfully slipped back through Zambia into Angola. Once inside, he renounced exile and, on the rebound, undertook to lead an internally-based insurgency of attrition against Portuguese colonial rule.

In due course, Savimbi's forces were challenged by rival anticolonial guerrillas. Equipped with Soviet arms, the MPLA infiltrated from Zambia into eastern Angola. Superior weaponry and training gave these MPLA units a distinct military advantage. They sought to parlay this advantage into a revolutionary ascendancy that would establish them as the sole contender for power in an independent Angola. In order to survive during this difficult period, Savimbi may have collaborated occasionally with the Portuguese, who viewed the MPLA as the more formidable threat. He tried repeatedly to form an alliance with the Frente Nacional de Libertação de Angola (FNLA) of Holden Roberto, whom he had renounced in 1964 as a pro-American tribalist. Rebuffed in these efforts, he and his movement persisted, with little outside notice or help, in a lonely bush insurgency.

With the military coup that toppled the Lisbon government of Marcello Caetano in 1974, the door to political decolonization in Angola seemed to open. Savimbi, who had always preferred and excelled in political as opposed to military strategy, seized the chance to win politically what lack of external support had made impossible militarily. With prospectively profitable wisdom, he suggested the need for a period of political education to prepare Angolans for free elections prior to independence and set out to organize broad political support.

Jonas Savimbi has long displayed a talent for discerning and telling people what they want to hear. As early as 1962, he wrote to American friends coupling pleas for financial aid with a pledge to help push communism out of Africa. In 1974–1975 he proved to be a spellbinding orator, effectively tailoring his remarks to his audience. On the one hand, Savimbi soothed the anxieties of Portuguese Angolans with assurances that he considered all those who had settled, let alone been born, in Angola to be bona fide Angolans. On the other hand, he promised black Angolans a new order under majority rule, free from domination by Portuguese-educated whites and *mestiços*. In 1975, *Le Monde*'s Gilbert Comte wrote: "Intelligent, intuitive, and gifted with great personal charm, [Savimbi offered] the anxious multitudes the reassuring words they so [wanted] to hear."

Despite Savimbi's evident moderation, political popularity, and Western leanings, the United States played a key role in blocking UNITA's bid for political power in the 1975–1976 period. In January 1975, when Angola was teetering on the edge of civil war, the Ford administration elected to authorize a covert grant of $300,000 to Holden Roberto's FNLA – whose strategy relied predominantly on high-risk military action. In its subsequent failure to lend diplomatic support to either Portuguese or collective African (Organization of African Unity) efforts to restrain external intervention (either Soviet or South African), promote reconciliation among Angolans, and assure neutrally supervised elections, the United States forfeited its opportunity to facilitate a peaceful transition to independence.

After the MPLA took control of the reins of the central government in 1976, Holden Roberto fled back to exile in Zaire (and ultimately France). Savimbi returned to the against-the-odds bush war of the preindependence period, continuing a long-term strategy designed to prove that the participation of UNITA is essential to any government that hopes to rule a peaceful Angola. Logistical support from South Africa, money from Saudi Arabia, and modest help from other states such as China and Morocco nourished his resistance. Finally, it was as David fighting the Goliath of Soviet-Cuban "imperialism" that he was discovered and lionized in the United States. Notably in conservative political circles that had shunned him and his cause during the days of anticolonial insurgency, he became the anti-Communist hope for expulsion of Soviet, and restoration of Western, influence in Angola.

Could there be a UNITA without Savimbi? Certainly the movement has capable second-tier leaders, and the basis for its political support extends to interests and grievances that do not rely solely on Savimbi's capacity to mobilize and command support. Yet UNITA's durability has rested in some measure on the sheer power of the Savimbi myth, his remarkable capacity to survive. It is impossible to know whether anyone else could effectively move up to fill the void that his loss would entail.

Tribalist or Racist?

In 1976, the year that the MPLA regime was accepted into the OAU and the United Nations as the legitimate government of Angola, a significant number of young central highlanders left their schools and families to follow UNITA into the wilderness. These politically conscious young people, mostly Ovimbundu, constituted a cadre of potential regional leadership, and their flight was thus a serious deprivation for the victorious MPLA. But did the exodus not confirm the essentially ethnic character of UNITA? Is UNITA not really a "tribalist" instrument of the Ovimbundu community that comprises up to 40 percent of Angola's population?

Nothing about UNITA is really that simple. In 1965, just prior to its founding, Savimbi wrote to the United Church Board for World Ministries setting forth the need for a new political movement to enlist the people of central and southern Angola (Ovimbundu, Chokwe, Ganguela, Ovambo) into the nationalist struggle. From the onset, the southern two-thirds of the country constituted UNITA's regional base. During the brief period (1974–1975) when UNITA could freely organize in northern areas, however, it was also able to attract support within MPLA (Mbundu)– and FNLA (Bakongo)-oriented communities. And in 1976, it was accompanied in its retreat back to the bush by a multiethnic leadership. Savimbi's principal lieutenant (since 1968), Miguel N'Zau Puna, comes from the northern, oil-rich enclave of Cabinda. In addition to veteran Ovimbundu guerrillas such as Chinese-trained Commander José Samuel Chiwale, UNITA's military leadership has included significant representation from other ethnic areas – e.g., French-educated António Vakulukuta (Ovambo) in the far south, and UNITA's former organizer in Zambia, Smart Chata (Chokwe), in the east. In short, though UNITA, unlike the MPLA, accepts ethnicity as a valid political variable, it is, itself, multiethnic.

UNITA's critics sometimes portray the movement as racist. One reason why UNITA, from its creation, displayed sharp distrust of the MPLA's commitment to multiracialism may have been that Portugal's harsh colonial policies belied and discredited an official doctrine of color-blind multiracialism that failed to mask the reality of white domination. Viewing the world through prisms of educational and economic disadvantage, "Unitists" dismissed MPLA multiracialism as a rationale that would enable *mestiços* and whites within its leadership ranks to assure their own form of elitist rule. UNITA tended, instead, to adopt a pragmatic form of Afrocentric populism, which was at once aggregative and demagogic. Thus, when it seemed as though Angola's more than 300,000 resident Portuguese would be participating in the creation of an independent state (1974–1975), UNITA actively recruited white membership. But in the same time period its spokesman told the American editor of *Black World* (October 1974 issue) that whites would be accepted as "visitors – nevermore as leaders" and that black American settlers would be welcomed in independent Angola.

Perceiving their own social experience in terms of racial exploitation, UNITA leaders espoused Pan-African solidarity, which they extended to include black Americans. In 1973, representatives from a black American liberation support group hiked deep into Angola to attend a UNITA congress which obligingly proclaimed "its militant and active solidarity with the African brothers and sisters in the Americas who are heroically fighting against imperialist oppression." UNITA named one of its military units the Black Panthers.

In 1976, last-minute efforts to recruit black Americans to help stave off defeat by the MPLA (*The Washington Post*, January 27, 1976) came to naught. Both before and to date, however, UNITA's public relations in the United States have been handled by Florence Tate and Associates of Washington, D.C. Florence Tate described herself in a 1976 interview as someone who for "nearly 20 years has played an active role in the civil rights, Black Power, and Pan-African socialist movements in the United States" and who knew "at first hand the lengths to which the U.S. will go to discredit and destroy that which it deems undesirable and cannot control." "Any U.S.-born African" with political experience, she argued, knows that U.S. policy toward Angola is based upon a globalist or "superpower view" of U.S. (not Angolan) interests. Because it does not act with genuine knowledge of what other people want for themselves, she concluded, the United States may intervene disastrously in support of an unpopular regime in Vietnam, then fail to assist a popularly supported UNITA in Angola. It will fail to understand that Angola is potentially "Russia's Vietnam" (*The Washington Post*, January 11, 1976).

An angry UNITA document of the same period entitled "Left/Right Counterfeit in Angola" similarly concluded: "The West found it safer and cheaper to deal with a predictable minority and dependent party like MPLA because it could influence MPLA through its détente partner, Russia, more effectively than it could influence a broad democratic front, a mass party like UNITA that would remain unpredictable and unmanageable as long as it drew its strength from popular support rather than a superpower."

Seen from the perspective of UNITA's black nationalism, the Soviets and Cubans represent an extension of white rule. After their deportation from Angola in 1977, the last two missionaries of the United Church of Canada described racial and political attitudes prevailing in the central district of Bie: "People were always noticing that UNITA's platform is for complete independence and not neocolonialism from either the East or West. A completely African society and government. Whites can stay provided they are willing to be under a Black government. This attracted support for UNITA. People felt that the Cubans running over them were just another white people taking the place of the Portuguese. Some said that if they had to have a foreign power in there they might as well have kept the Portuguese."

Capitalist or Socialist?

Although wishfully depicted by some Americans as a pro-Western champion of free enterprise, Jonas Savimbi has consistently declared himself an exponent of African socialism. Asked in late 1975 by American journalist Robin

Wright to describe his politics, Savimbi responded that he was neither Communist nor capitalist. Socialism – democratic, not "extremist" socialism – is the "only answer" for Angola, he said, for the country's new leaders ought not to become "exploiters of the people." As for foreign investors, Savimbi declared himself against nationalization but for tough bargaining and contracts so as to insure a proper share of corporate profits for the public treasury.

As the principal architect of UNITA doctrine, Savimbi has persistently called for a cooperative socialist society able to accommodate Angola's African cultural heritage and create a new "liberated man." As recently as December 1982, he told a group of Western correspondents that he is "not a capitalist" because he does not intend to exploit his people. On the other hand, a recently distributed UNITA document, *National Economic Reconstruction in Angola: The Challenge and the Approach*, avoids the word "socialist" and dwells instead on the merits of "realistic socio-economic analysis" as compared to "the sloganeering, Marxist rhetoric and poor performance of East European 'cooperantes'" who have brought only "economic disaster." The document goes on to describe both public and private enterprise as appropriate and suggests that: "In order to encourage Angolan nationals to undertake business initiatives [a UNITA] government would set up appropriate technical, financial, and research assistance programs for small and medium enterprises." Whether this statement represents a shift away from earlier commitments or merely an avoidance of words offensive to Americans, UNITA's economics might be more safely described as nationalist and pragmatic than as socialist.

Natural Affinities and Unnatural Expediencies

Economic doctrine represents but one of many areas in which UNITA's original inclinations or intentions seem to have been at least temporarily modified, deflected, or compromised in response to perceived political necessity. Of special relevance to the search for diplomatic solutions for the turmoil in Angola and Namibia are UNITA's fluctuating relationships with Namibia's SWAPO and South Africa.

SWAPO's traditional political base lies in the Ovambo community, which straddles the Angola-Namibia boundary. Since access to Ovamboland from SWAPO's exile headquarters in Zambia lies across southeast Angola, geography has provided a basis for UNITA-SWAPO collaboration. For a full decade, this collaboration was close and extensive. It started in 1965 at Dar es Salaam, where Savimbi established such intimate relations with SWAPO leaders that he used their post office box as his own address. That same year an initial cadre of 12 UNITA guerrillas began training with SWAPO at a military base in China. Describing the decade of collaboration that followed, a UNITA spokesman later wrote: "During this time, SWAPO was able to reach Namibian territory to fight the South African racists by transiting UNITA-held territory. UNITA provided food, refuge, and training – particularly for SWAPO soldiers who had received Soviet training which did not prepare them for successful guerrilla warfare." In response, South African helicopters transported their own and Portuguese assault forces in attacks against both Angolan and SWAPO guerrillas across a broad zone of southeast Angola.

In 1973, the leader of the MPLA, Dr. Agostinho Neto, complained to Zambia that SWAPO was shipping arms and Zambian travel documents to UNITA under the false pretext that UNITA controlled the "vital passage" of southeast Angola. The UNITA-SWAPO alliance managed to survive pressure from the Soviet Union, which was supporting SWAPO and the MPLA (but not UNITA) with arms. Sharing ethno-populist affinities that distanced them from the left-wing multiracialism of the MPLA, UNITA and SWAPO continued to cooperate even after the Portuguese coup of 1974. Ovambo youths, who slipped northward across the Angolan border to join SWAPO, were fed and sheltered by UNITA. And according to UNITA sources, when Savimbi and his colleagues moved into urban areas to campaign (1974–1975), they also shared vehicles, medical supplies, office facilities, and weapons with SWAPO, thereby enabling the latter to step up political and military activities against South Africa. Collaboration even persisted for a while after South Africa intervened in Angola, but came to an end, according to UNITA, in 1976 after Cuban forces drove south into areas of SWAPO activity, and the Namibians were obliged by their own national interests to lead the Cubans to UNITA camps and to work with the MPLA.

It is possible to read the evidence somewhat differently. Already in late 1974, UNITA's representative in Luanda seemed to be putting some distance between the two groups by implying to *The Star* (Johannesburg) that it was up to Namibians to fight for their own independence, leaving Angola free to establish relations with South Africa based on mutual "respect and noninterference." In mid-1975, as it became evident that power in Angola would be taken by force of arms rather than an electoral contest all neutral observers picked UNITA to win, a sense of desperation seized UNITA leadership.

As he watched Soviet arms and Cuban instructors building the MPLA into a certain winner, Jonas Savimbi turned to South Africa. He was quoted in the *Windhoek Advertiser* (June 12, 1975) as saying that Angola faced problems of such nature as to preclude it from assisting SWAPO. Impressed by South African military power, convinced that NATO countries shared South Africa's determination to keep Angola free from Soviet influence, and apparently believing that South Africa's policy of détente toward such states as Zambia, Zaire, and even Mozambique had reduced the liabilities of association with Pretoria, Savimbi took the plunge. According to American intelligence sources, UNITA undertook to provide information on the location of SWAPO bases as a quid pro quo for South African arms, instructors, and commandos. For reasons that were political rather than military, South African forces stopped short of taking Luanda. Then, in the face of a growing Cuban expeditionary force that had been given international (especially African) legitimacy by the threat of South African conquest, the South African military drew back into Namibia from whence it has continued to provide UNITA with logistical support and arms. UNITA and SWAPO guerrillas were left to fight for control over sparse cattle, food, and water resources in the barren south of Angola.

Despite all this, the affinities which underlay the long operational alliance between UNITA and SWAPO still persist. UNITA sources have recently quoted Savimbi as saying that relations between the two movements have moved back from a state of fratricidal war to one of distant cordiality (their soldiers avoid contact) and that he would expect UNITA to have good relations with a future SWAPO government in Namibia. Despite continuing reports of UNITA-SWAPO clashes, MPLA government officials are reported to be concerned about the possibility that a SWAPO government might, indeed, ultimately align itself with UNITA.

In assessing UNITA, one must reckon with both political preferences and Savimbi's willingness to compromise, even wantonly. These are important considerations in any assessment of the possible consequences of either integrating UNITA into or keeping UNITA out of the government of Angola. While Savimbi and his colleagues prefer Western to Eastern associations, the record is clear that in 1964, as his partnership with Roberto was fraying, he made a bid for Soviet support during a journey to Moscow seldom mentioned in UNITA circles. Soviet terms were for him to join the MPLA. He refused, choosing instead to look elsewhere for means to ensure him and his supporters survival as an independent political force. More acceptable was China's offer of military training and some arms in return for rhetorical celebration of Maoist achievements and Soviet failures.

Savimbi and his colleagues would prefer to govern Angola alone. But they have periodically sought a common front or entente with the MPLA from the time UNITA was

officially founded in 1966. When the MPLA finally exhibited interest in a two-party alliance (against the FNLA) during bilateral talks at Lisbon in August 1975, the United
States reportedly interceded to dissuade UNITA from such
an accord. In a 1979 interview with Charles Cobb of *Africa
News*, Savimbi referred to the MPLA as "patriots" who also
"fought for the independence of our country" and indicated
that he would not even make the withdrawal of Cuban
troops a precondition for negotiations with the MPLA. But
he also acknowledged that the MPLA was unlikely to talk
until, in a year or two, it had finally come to accept that it
could not militarily eliminate UNITA. Since then, UNITA
guerrillas have extended their activities northward into the
Mbundu country of Malange.

For the MPLA in 1983, it may be difficult to decide
whether a politically supple Savimbi is more dangerous
within or without. For the Soviet Union, the entry of
UNITA into the Luanda government would, like the departure of the Cubans, constitute an embarrassing political
setback. For South Africa, a role for UNITA in Luanda
would vindicate the earlier decision to assure UNITA's survival. And for the Reagan administration, UNITA participation in the government would be perceived as a political
gain, even though American corporate investors have been
positive in their view of the MPLA government as pragmatic and honest.

As for Savimbi and UNITA, they could be expected, if
brought into the government, to league together with black
nationalists in the MPLA in quest of expanded power. If
kept out, they could be expected to fight on, forcing the
retention of Cuban or other foreign garrisons. By drawing
upon stockpiled arms and Ovimbundu support, UNITA
might even survive a cutoff of South African aid in the
eventuality of an Angolan-South African cease-fire accord.
Meanwhile, the advice of their Chinese mentors that the
march to power may be long and tortuous remains a guiding principle for UNITA as it pursues the politics of survival into an uncharted future.

2

A Quarter Century of War

John A. Marcum

December 1984

"The principal element in the deterioration of [U.S.] relations with the Soviet Union," Secretary of State Henry Kissinger told a Washington news conference in April 1976, "is Soviet actions in Angola." In retrospect, the unanticipated and massive Soviet-Cuban intervention in Angola's civil war did represent an important watershed. The dramatic projection of Soviet military power and political influence into southern Africa, followed by the military interventions in Ethiopia and Afghanistan, marked the beginning of the end of superpower détente. However, the general assumption that Soviet-Cuban military support had definitively secured the rule over all of Angola of its beneficiary, the MPLA, proved premature.

Today, nearly a quarter of a century after the outbreak of anticolonial insurgency and a decade after the military coup in Lisbon that resulted in the hurried liquidation of the Portuguese empire, Angola continues to be ravaged by war. A host of external powers, large and small, continues to be involved in the protracted competition for control over a country whose natural resources could provide the basis for a prosperous future were it ever to enjoy a period of social peace. For most Angolans, political independence has meant until now only increased deprivation and insecurity.

The MPLA: Yesterday and Today

Any movement or coalition of movements that attained power in Angola in 1975 would have faced horrendous difficulties. The legacy of Portuguese colonial rule was political inexperience, 85 to 90 percent illiteracy, and communal division. Civil war and the abrupt departure of nearly 350,000 resident Portuguese (with their trucks as well as their skills) had laid waste to a belatedly developing economy. Angola entered independence in a destructive whirlwind of fratricidal violence.

The MPLA did have the advantage of setting out to construct and govern the new polity of Angola from the heart of its own ethno-regional stronghold. The new regime was a product of Luanda-Mbundu society, that 25 percent of the Angolan population most influenced by centuries of Portuguese rule. It was in this "central society" and other urban centers integrated within the colonial economy, as distinguished from the more remote but majoritarian "tributary societies" of peasants and herders, that economic and cultural protest first developed into organized anticolonialism in the 1950s and 1960s.

The MPLA derived from a galaxy of small urban groups, centered around the person and family of Dr. Agostinho Neto, which united in 1956. Some of these factions were founded or influenced by Portuguese and Brazilian Marxists (teachers, civil servants, commercial employees); one of the groups was reportedly a tiny (just over a dozen members) Partido Comunista de Angola (PCA).

During the period of anticolonial insurgency, the MPLA carefully maintained its formal status as an eclectic front. Its leaders rejected proposals to convert it into a "revolutionary party" until such time as a solid nucleus of ideologically trained cadres could be prepared. MPLA ideology did, however, manifest traces of Marxism, with a consistent emphasis on egalitarian (class), multiracial, and anti-imperialist themes; and over time political and military cadres were trained in the Soviet Union, Eastern Europe, and Cuba. Soviet spokesmen openly expressed optimism that assisting the MPLA would spread "the idea of socialism and revolutionary anticolonialist ideology."

As Portuguese authority crumbled in the 19 months following the 1974 Lisbon coup, the MPLA simultaneously (1) attracted new cadres of educated blacks and *mestiços* into its ranks and (2) organized among dislocated, ex-peasant slum dwellers who had migrated into the towns during the war-related economic growth of the 1960s and early 1970s. The gulf between these social strata constituted — and still constitutes — an inherent obstacle to MPLA cohesion. Before the first government of the People's Republic of Angola (PRA) could even secure its authority over the "central society" of the Luanda-Mbundu region, Nito Alves, an ambitious organizer of MPLA (*poder popular*) action groups in Luanda, tried to parlay racial cleavage into personal political power. Moving swiftly to exploit popular discontent over food shortages, Alves and his black-oriented *fraccionistas* blamed economic distress on the mismanagement and ideological laxity of an administration that they said had accorded an unduly prominent, elite class role to whites and *mestiços*.

Thwarted within the MPLA organization, Alves and his supporters attempted a coup in May 1977. Although they failed, several prominent party leaders were killed and the episode revealed the MPLA's vulnerability to racial demagoguery and economic distress. It also demonstrated the qualified nature of the MPLA's external support, for Alves was a voluble champion of closer ties with the Soviet Union. The official inquiry into the aborted coup acknowledged that he and his followers had managed to undermine confidence in the MPLA government among diplomats from "friendly countries," apparently including officials of the Soviet embassy, where Alves was a frequent visitor. The Soviets failed to provide the government of President Agostinho Neto with advance warning of Alves's intentions.

The experience left the MPLA shaken, wary, and distrustful even of external allies. The Alves affair helps to explain why in 1984 an externally dependent and militarily beleaguered MPLA government may approach negotiations with those who are not even nominally "friends," notably Americans or South Africans, with a keen sense of suspicion and insecurity.

Underlying MPLA distrust of American intentions is a long history of negative experience. It includes the rebuff of MPLA overtures for U.S. assistance (in contrast to supportive U.S./NATO ties to Portugal) during the anticolonial struggle. At the time of the civil war in 1975, the United States provided substantial though ineffective assistance to the "anti-Communist" movements competing with the MPLA for power in Angola. According to senior MPLA officials, it was bitter reaction to this intervention, coupled with that of South Africa and Zaire, that generated irresistible internal pressure for a more rapid and radical embrace of Eastern-style socialism than otherwise would have occurred.

The MPLA convened its first postindependence national congress in December 1977. At this gathering, the decision was made to become officially a Marxist-Leninist party. Under the name of MPLA-Partido do Trabalho, the party dedicated its relatively small and indoctrinated membership (25,000 members, plus aspirants, as of 1982) to work toward the construction of a new society based on "scientific socialism."

Under both Agostinho Neto and his successor, José Eduardo dos Santos, the MPLA was to manifest a considerable measure of economic pragmatism. According to one sympathetic Western account, the MPLA sought to avoid a transitional "capitalist phase" of development for fear that it would "result in the kind of anarchy and corruption typical of Zaire, Ivory Coast or Zambia" where "international monopoly capitalism creamed off the important profits" and "small-scale national operatives" manipulated the rest into their pockets. (Michael Wolfers and Jane Bergerol, *Angola in the Front Line* [London: Zed Press, 1983], p. 190.)

But the MPLA was also quick to form a partnership with the Gulf Oil Corporation, whose Cabinda operation keeps the economy afloat. And the United States, despite the fact that it has never recognized the MPLA regime, imports some $600 million worth of Angolan oil annually, rendering Angola its third-ranking trade partner in sub-Saharan Africa.

In general, the PRA's economic record has been abysmal. Agricultural production collapsed when Portuguese traders crucial to its marketing fled in 1975. Some 80 percent of the commercial food supply must be imported. Coffee harvests are still less than half of preindependence levels. Diamond mining and trade have been plagued with corruption born of economic desperation and low civil morale. Oil exports provide 75 percent of the state income, but probably over half of the oil revenue is spent on military and security items instead of being plowed back into basic economic development. A significant part of the outlay for security is the payment for the maintenance of some 20,000 to 25,000 Cuban troops and another 10,000 Cuban, Soviet, and East European technicians who protect the government and keep it functioning. According to Minister of Planning Lopo do Nascimento, Angolan payments cover food and housing but, contrary to Western intelligence sources, do not include salaries for Cuban soldiers.

The Soviet Union has shown no inclination to provide the sort of massive economic assistance that might enable Angola to break out of its economic morass, although it has helped with some specific projects. For example, it agreed in 1982 to participate in the design and construction of the Kapande hydroelectric station on the Cuanza River. (In at least one economic sector, coastal fishing, Soviet activities have been essentially exploitative and profoundly resented.)

In sum, the hope and promise of independence have given way to frustration as security needs devour the resources and creative energies of the country. How and why has this happened?

What the MPLA Faced

As the inadequately trained, ill-disciplined soldiers of UNITA retreated into the vast emptiness of southeastern Angola in February 1976, it seemed unlikely that they would be an important factor in the future of Angola. The bitterness of their retreat was matched only by its futile savagery. As they withdrew, UNITA forces slaughtered known MPLA officials and supporters — 235 in Huambo alone.

By midyear, however, UNITA's resilient leader, Jonas Savimbi, had regrouped his disheveled army in the southeastern savannah. Joined by a flow of young educated Ovimbundu from the populous central plateau, Savimbi and his still intact, multiethnic roster of political-military lieutenants returned to their pre-1974 roles as against-the-odds bush guerrillas. Crucial to their resilience was the military training at Namibian camps provided to UNITA's remnant forces by the South African Defense Force (SADF).

If the MPLA was to insure that neither UNITA nor the shattered forces of Holden Roberto's northern, Bakongo-based FNLA would ever reemerge as serious contenders for political power, the regime had to reach out beyond its own Luanda-Mbundu constituency and attract active participation from all sectors of the country within the life and structures of the PRA. The efforts toward this end were more successful among the Bakongo, who compose roughly 20 percent of Angola's population, than within UNITA's power base.

The FNLA

Like UNITA, the FNLA managed to reestablish a small-scale guerrilla operation in areas where it had been active before independence, in this instance the rolling forest country of the north. But the MPLA moved expeditiously to integrate Kikongo-speakers into the political and economic life of the PRA. Illustrative of this policy of co-option was the ethnic evolution of the MPLA's powerful 11-member Political Bureau. In October 1976, it consisted of six Mbundu, three mestiços, one Bakongo, and one Cabindan. Three years later, this had changed to four Mbundu, two mestiços, three Bakongo, and two Cabindans. Co-option extended to bringing a few former FNLA leaders, such as onetime FNLA Vice President Emanuel Kunzika, into responsible administrative positions within the government.

So long as FNLA remnants could operate freely from their traditional training and supply bases in Zaire, however, they could be troublesome. After two incursions into Zaire's Shaba province by Katangan exiles in Angola had threatened to provoke a general disintegration of Zairian central authority, Angola's Agostinho Neto reached an understanding with Zaire's Mobutu Sese Seko in July 1978. In return for curbing the Katangans and encouraging their repatriation, Neto eventually persuaded Mobutu to close down FNLA bases and expel Holden Roberto. In 1979, Roberto, already discredited by his incompetent leadership during the latter stages of the civil war (against military advice, he had marched his FNLA army headlong into the withering rocket and artillery fire of MPLA and Cuban forces in a desperate effort to capture Luanda before independence), flew off to exile in Paris.

Beginning in August 1980, an anti-Roberto FNLA-Comitê Militar de Resistência de Angola (COMIRA) undertook to recreate an exile political structure in Zaire and to organize anti-MPLA politico-military operations in northeastern Angola (Uige-Malange). As a consequence of the Neto-Mobutu rapprochement, however, FNLA-COMIRA's top leadership was also forced to leave Zaire.

In September 1983, when it seemed that at least the FNLA had ceased to be a player in Angola's internal conflict, Holden Roberto resurfaced – in the United States. Stating that he was sponsored by a little-known organization called the Jefferson Foundation, Roberto began a speaking and lobbying tour that reached from California to

Washington. Asserting that 5,000 to 7,000 armed FNLA
guerrillas loyal to him were fighting in northern Angola, he
appealed for financial support, warned against U.S. recognition of the PRA, and denounced what he termed an MPLA-
Cuban plot to perpetuate Cuban domination even in the
eventuality of a withdrawal of Cuban troops from Angola.
In his view, this "conspiracy" is reflected in 1984 legislation
that authorizes the Angolan People's Assembly to confer
citizenship on selected foreigners. (The reference is to Article 6 of [Nationality] Law 2/84 [February 7, 1984], which
reads: "The People's Assembly is authorized to confer
Angolan nationality on foreign citizens who have contributed relevant service to the country.")

Despite Roberto's efforts to garner support, his pretensions to leadership were dismissed as an exile's fantasy by
most observers as his visit to the United States lingered on
into its second year and news came that two of his former
top lieutenants had defected to the MPLA in Luanda. All
told, the MPLA has managed to co-opt or see exiled much
of its old northern opposition—including fractious groups
seeking independence for the oil-rich Cabinda enclave.

UNITA: A Different Story

The MPLA has not enjoyed comparable success with regard to UNITA and the central-southern "tributary societies" (Ovimbundu, Chokwe, Ganguela, Ambo) that constitute UNITA's political support base. Although the
Ovimbundu alone amount to something over a third of the
population, their representation in the MPLA Political Bureau remains nil and in the Central Committee less than 10
percent.

According to party officials, the uneven MPLA presence in the provinces is mainly attributable to uneven development of local social forces and political awareness. These
officials acknowledge, however, that excessive centraliza-
tion of "the state apparatus" delayed the implantation of

the MPLA outside of "detribalized" (urban) areas. And as a partial explanation of UNITA's regional following, MPLA information secretary Roberto de Almeida has cited UNITA efforts to stir up old prejudices against the north where Ovimbundu and others were previously sent by the Portuguese to work as conscript labor on coffee plantations and in factories. Although "Angolans had nothing to do with these practices," he laments, it is still possible to exploit the resultant prejudice and distrust existing among Angola's different ethnic groups.

Perhaps influenced by the long-standing MPLA disdain for racial and ethnic loyalties, MPLA military commanders flush with victory in the civil war of 1975–1976 assured President Neto that remaining "pockets" of UNITA resistance "would be cleaned out in no time." In the estimation of seasoned Angola specialist Gerald J. Bender, the inability of the Luanda government to revive agricultural production and to provide essential goods and services to the vast outreaches of central and southern Angola was the most decisive factor in the "maintenance and growth" of support for UNITA. The overconfident MPLA also underestimated Jonas Savimbi's political skills—rhetorical, aggregative, manipulative. And it suffered from a failure to foresee the nature and magnitude of the South African response to an MPLA decision to permit the South West Africa People's Organization (SWAPO) to establish training camps, supply routes, and logistical support bases on Angolan soil.

A less noted factor in the survival of UNITA is the doctrinal rigidity with which the MPLA initially approached religious affairs. Ignoring the close historical relationship between the development of Angolan nationalism and the educational activities of colonially repressed Protestant missions, MPLA ideologues mounted a hard-line, Marxist-Leninist attack on Angolan churches, Protestant and Catholic alike. The result was to convert churches into an organizational focal point of opposition. A partial exception was the Methodist Church, centered in the Mbundu region and having historical ties (Agostinho Neto's father was a Methodist pastor) to the MPLA.

In December 1982, the MPLA fired the principal orchestrator of the antireligion campaign – the party secretary for ideological affairs, Ambrosio Lukoki (a Bakongo) – and relaxed its negative policies on religion. But the damage had been done. And although President dos Santos stated in a 1984 interview that the MPLA is open to all Angolans "without distinction of race, tribe, or religious belief," the fact is that MPLA party membership is denied to church members ("believers"). Savimbi, a product of Protestant upbringing (United Church of Christ and United Church of Canada), and UNITA have thus been assured of sympathy among urban congregations and the active support of the Church of Christ in the Bush. There are also supportive links to North American Protestants.

Firm evidence of UNITA's survival gradually emerged in reports of ambushes and sabotage, especially along the Benguela railroad, and in increasingly frequent visits to UNITA camps and "must" interviews with Savimbi by Western journalists. Before independence, UNITA had been the least effective of the Angolan nationalist movements in the area of public relations, but this was reversed through Savimbi's growing flair for dealing with the media and through the help of Florence Tate and Associates of Washington, D.C.

Beginning in August 1981, devastating annual incursions by the SADF deep into Angola served more than the stated purpose of wiping out SWAPO raiders and bases. The South Africans mauled FAPLA (Forças Armadas Populares de Libertação de Angola), the MPLA's Soviet- and Cuban-trained army of some 35,000, backed up by perhaps 50,000 local militia. They destroyed communications, economic infrastructure, entire towns; provided large hauls of Soviet weapons to UNITA; and demoralized FAPLA soldiers, thereby facilitating UNITA initiatives to expand the range of its operations. For the PRA, the costs were enormous. By itself, UNITA's closure of the Benguela railroad to

Zambian and Zairian copper ore represents a loss of up to $100 million a year in transit fees. MPLA officials bitterly complain that UNITA activities have hampered efforts to reconstruct the country's economy.

FAPLA has countered with intensified defense tactics, e.g., forced resettlement and mining the approaches to exposed towns. The Soviets have provided the PRA with increasingly sophisticated weapons, most recently mobile radar installations, antiaircraft guns, MiG-23s, and Mi-24 helicopter gunships. The PRA pays in hard currency for most of these arms, although given the extremity of its circumstances in the wake of devastating South African and UNITA military activity, the Soviet Union has reportedly eased and lengthened the terms of payment during the past year. FAPLA's dominance of the air is what deters UNITA from holding the towns that it captures, but the government's resort to motorized patrols (using Soviet tanks and armored cars) seems a questionable choice of response to UNITA's attack-at-dawn, blow-it-up, pillage, and melt-away tactics. The rebels have infiltrated north from their Cuando Cubango and Moxico bases, spreading along the Zambia and Zaire borders. UNITA strikes in places as far-flung as Sumbe (Novo Redondo) on the coast, which it held for some 36 hours; Luanda harbor, where it claims to have planted the mines that damaged two ships; and the Lomaum dam (near Alto Catumbelo), where it damaged Huambo's principal source of electricity.

Intent upon convincing the international community that no settlement is possible without its participation, UNITA has recently adopted a strategy of dramatic, sometimes brutal psychological warfare. It captures foreign advisors and technicians (Soviet, Czechoslovak, Portuguese, British, even U.S.), marches them hundreds of miles through desolate terrain to its "provisional capital" of Jamba in the southeastern corner of Angola, and there releases them at theatrical ceremonies attended obligatorily by official representatives, and often press, from the hostages' states. Although the Western media has not labeled this hostage-gathering as "terrorism," the term seems unavoidable when reporting UNITA ferocity in urban centers. How does one differentiate between the truck-bombing of the U.S. Embassy in Beirut and the April 1984 UNITA operation in which a jeep loaded with explosives was driven to a seven-story building in Huambo, killing some 100 to 200 persons?

Savimbi has succeeded in assuring that he cannot be ignored. UNITA's hardy resourcefulness – combined with Moroccan military training, Saudi and other Middle Eastern oil money, Zambian and Zairian willingness to ignore border crossings, possibly some Israeli expertise, and, above all, South African nurturing (crucial food and diesel supplies) – have all contributed to UNITA's development into a complex, self-propelled organization which might well survive a South African-PRA accommodation that sharply reduced South African assistance.

UNITA's "regular" forces number some 15,000 (Savimbi claims 20,000 "regular army troops" plus 20,000 "guerrillas," and says that he receives funding of as much as $60 to $70 million annually "from many Arab friends"). Soviet observers, among others, view the role of Zaire as increasingly significant. The Luanda government has given President Mobutu fair warning, however, that he would risk retaliation in the form of a possible third Katangan incursion into Shaba were Zaire to become a major arms channel and logistical support base for UNITA.

An MPLA-UNITA Coalition?

Jonas Savimbi manifested considerable nervousness following South Africa's February 1984 agreement with the PRA to pull its troops out of southern Angola in return for a PRA ban on SWAPO activity in the area. His public response was to speak confidently of U.S., Portuguese, and French understanding of the "motives of UNITA's struggle," and to warn that UNITA is the "best ally South Africa can have in these parts." Above all, Savimbi pressed the proposition that the South African and U.S. policy goal of a Cuban withdrawal from Angola cannot take place unless and until the MPLA brings itself to accept a political accord (presumably a coalition) with UNITA. "The key," he insists, "is to bring the MPLA and UNITA together so that the Cubans can leave."

The MPLA—embittered by years of bloodshed, unsure of its own rural support (especially the loyalty of traditional chiefs and uneducated peasants who have been cultivated by UNITA), and distrustful of Savimbi's political ambition, daring, drive, and close ties with South Africa—has rebuffed UNITA's overtures. President dos Santos has been consistent and categorical: the MPLA will not talk with those who "steal, pillage, and carry out the wishes of their South African masters. With such enemies, no dialogue is possible. We can only fight them." For the MPLA, Jonas Savimbi's dramatic appearance at President P. W. Botha's inauguration in September constituted a puzzling public confirmation of his alliance with South Africa and further justification for the "no talk" stance.

Does this unwillingness to consider negotiations with Savimbi or his top lieutenants necessarily preclude any international agreement that would encompass a major pullback and reduction of the number of Cuban troops now in Angola? Does the wide range and increasing scope of UNITA military action not require the continued presence of the Cubans? Possibly not. Because they perceive UNITA as essentially a creature of South African logistical, material, and technical (specialists in sabotage) assistance, MPLA leaders appear to believe that a limited agreement with South Africa entailing a mutual withdrawal of South African and Cuban forces and an end to South African assistance to UNITA would enable them over a period of a few years to push back and marginalize UNITA insurgency. Savimbi's November 9, 1984 convocation of over 40 journalists at his Jamba headquarters to warn that UNITA must be factored into any settlement suggests that he may share this apparent MPLA perception and fear future abandonment by South Africa.

MPLA reasoning seems to be based upon a higher estimate of its army's morale and skills and a lower estimate of those of its adversary than some observers in Luanda and elsewhere believe justified. Central to this reasoning is the assumption that an Angolan-South African accord along the lines currently being discussed, if coupled with U.S. diplomatic recognition and an increased inflow of Western development capital, would enable the MPLA government within reasonable time to deliver the goods and services needed to win the loyalty of war-weary peasants and, eventually, the civilian and military followers of Jonas Savimbi.

Some Soviet analysts have expressed the compatible view that, after many years in the bush, the more "responsible" elements within UNITA may be becoming disenchanted with what can never be a winning strategy, while Savimbi may be wedded to the romanticism of a dead-end guerrilla struggle. These Soviet analysts speculate that there may well be a split in UNITA ranks as it becomes clear that (1) any escalation of UNITA military activity will be met by a firm resolve on the part of the MPLA and its external allies to defend the integrity of the PRA, and that (2) Savimbi's continued presence as leader represents a serious obstacle to an otherwise feasible accommodation. In this connection, it is noteworthy that Savimbi is accused by detractors of authoritarian tendencies; they point to his dismissal of previously important lieutenants, such as former foreign secretary Jorge Sangumba, as indicative of an inability to tolerate independent spirits. Journalists who make the journey to Jamba seldom report the words or names of anyone other than Savimbi.

Should Savimbi make good on his public predictions that UNITA will carry the war to the heart of Luanda, it is not unlikely that, in the words of a Western diplomat in Kinshasa, "the Cubans and Russians [would] just up the stake." One thing seems indisputable. As of late 1984, Savimbi's UNITA had become a crucial factor, though a nonparticipant, in the diplomatic negotiations aimed at withdrawal of Cuban troops from Angola and independence for Namibia. MPLA insistence on a cessation of South African assistance to UNITA as a part of any such agreement posed a major test of South African intentions.

Soviet Stakes

If, despite whatever Angola's 7 to 8 million people might hope, there seems to be little likelihood that the MPLA will negotiate with UNITA, it is also unlikely that the Soviet Union and Cuba would stand by idly should UNITA forces threaten to engulf Luanda. It does not necessarily follow, however, that Soviet strategic interests in Angola are more than modest. Although Soviet aircraft perform routine surveillance flights over the South Atlantic from Angolan airfields and Soviet naval vessels utilize Angolan ports, the Soviet presence is limited and has been kept clear of any direct confrontation with South African forces.

The USSR has engaged its prestige in Angola, however, and a sharp loss of influence or a Cuban troop withdrawal as a result of military action by South African-backed rebels would involve a serious loss of face. Moscow's political and ideological investment in the MPLA covers nearly three decades. Sour Soviet experiences with earlier "African socialist" regimes (notably Ghana, Guinea, Mali, and Somalia) have not yet been repeated with those professing Marxism which came to power via armed insurgency in former Portuguese colonies. When President dos Santos visited Moscow in May 1983, Soviet Communist Party head and President Yuri Andropov specifically welcomed the steadfastness ("invariable course") of the MPLA in "defending revolutionary gains and creating the foundations of a socialist society." The Soviet Union, he affirmed, "will be firmly on the side of the People's Republic of Angola in the defense of its sovereignty, independence, and territorial integrity."

Indeed, the Soviet Union obligated itself to do so by signing a Treaty of Friendship and Cooperation with Angola in 1976. The military clause of that treaty pledges that the two governments will strengthen their mutual defense capabilities by developing "cooperation in the military sphere" as circumstances make appropriate. This did not, however, preclude a solid measure of prudence. It is interesting to note that Angolan MiGs and gunships have never attacked Jamba.

Soviet writings portray the PRA as a "socialist-oriented" government currently traversing a preparatory "people's democratic revolution" phase "during which conditions will be created for a transition to the stage of socialist changes." They stress the importance of the MPLA's status as a "Marxist-Leninist party" determined to "embark on the path of socialist construction."

Soviet analysts divide African countries with a "socialist orientation" into two categories. The first is composed of states where "power is wielded by mass revolutionary-democratic parties, which adhere to revolutionary but at the same time petty-bourgeois ideology"; these include states such as Tanzania and Algeria. The second and higher category is composed of states where "vanguard parties of the working people standing on Marxist-Leninist positions" are leading the development of socialist societies. Ideally, these states are expected to achieve a "wider and more profound range of revolutionary transformations embracing all or almost all spheres of social life." The foreign policies of this more advanced subgroup of "socialist-oriented" countries, it is hoped, will be "based on recognition of the principles of proletarian internationalism and on the desire for closer cooperation with the Soviet Union and other socialist states and with the world Communist and workers' movement."

While it is an official "given" that the vanguard MPLA will be guided by Marxist-Leninist principles, the details (country-specific qualities) of Angolan socialism are, according to veteran MPLA party leader Lúcio Lara, yet to be determined. They are to be worked out pragmatically. Luandan leadership acknowledges the crucial contributions of its Communist "allies" in military and security affairs. But it insists that the People's Republic of Angola is no one's satellite. It adamantly denies allegations by critics that Soviet, East German, and Cuban advisors really run key government ministries. President José Eduardo dos Santos speaks warmly of "low cost," multifaceted assistance by Cuban teachers, doctors, civil engineers, and agronomists who "understand" the "sort of society we wish to build." When asked earlier this year about Angolan-Soviet relations, dos Santos noted suggestively that "relations between parties and peoples do not always develop without a hitch" but then concluded that recent visits to the Soviet Union and other socialist states had given him "the impression that our present problems are [now] better understood."

In the economic sphere, it is Western, not Eastern, expertise and capital that is becoming increasingly prominent. In addition to the revenue-generating role of Western oil companies such as Gulf and Texaco, West European involvement is expanding in many sectors. French aid is helping to revive coffee production and marketing; an Austrian firm (Austro-Mineral) has restarted iron ore production at Kassinga; Spanish assistance is helping to resuscitate the fishing industry of Namibe (Moçâmedes); and Swedish bankers are advising the National Bank of Angola on the management of its debt structure (international, largely short-term indebtedness was officially estimated at the outset of 1984 to be $2.2 billion and rapidly rising). The desire for increased Western ties extends from capital and technology to education. The rector of the formative University of Angola, along with other educators, evidences eagerness for diplomatic negotiations to open the door to scholarly exchanges with the United States.

The Soviets nonetheless continue to have important stakes in Angola. Faced with a sudden decline or total reversal of their role, they would have to consider whether to respond with a massive infusion of weapons and surrogate troops (Cuban or other). Their decision might depend upon whether they were presented with the possibility of an "honorable" resolution. Assuming that the drain of war on Soviet, as well as Cuban, South African, and, most important, MPLA human and material resources provides an incentive to find a way out, attentiveness to face, sensitivities, *amour-propre* becomes critical. Above all, the Soviets seem determined in Africa as elsewhere to be seen and treated as a major power, whose interest in and relations with the continent have the same legitimacy as those of the United States.

The Future

The PRA's evident dual desire to break out of past isolation (more Western journalists are to be allowed in) and to establish its authority throughout the country does not suggest a willingness to pursue these goals in the manner of Mozambique. It is not prepared to negotiate a comprehensive Nkomati Accord of "nonaggression and good neighborliness" with South Africa. Unlike Mozambique, Angola has no common border with South Africa or related need to enter into close economic association. For the same reason — no common border — the PRA rejects the notion of following Mozambique's example of breaking off long-standing ties with the African National Congress (ANC). (The sporting of *Libertar Mandela* T-shirts in Luanda is accompanied by rumors of an ANC military camp somewhere in the interior.) And by insisting on implementation of UN Security Council Resolution 435 on Namibia as part of any international troop disengagement agreement, the PRA hopes to assure that SWAPO will have clear access to a political victory at the Namibian polls. Of late, mobile conventional units of SWAPO have been increasing that movement's stock with the MPLA by engaging in what is reported to be the most effective fighting being conducted against UNITA guerrillas in central Angola.

In sum, the PRA is as determined to resist the "humiliation" of a sweeping Nkomati-style accord as it is to resist negotiating with Jonas Savimbi's UNITA. Accordingly, even if U.S. diplomatic efforts to broker an Angolan-South African agreement should lead to Cuban-South African troop disengagements and independence for Namibia (a big if), Angolan-South African relations are likely to remain minimal and wary and the MPLA-UNITA contest will likely continue its sanguinary course. Tragically for all its people, the peace that foreign diplomats, economists, businessmen, and scholars see as essential for the reconstruction and development of Angola is not yet in sight.

3

United States Options in Angola

John A. Marcum

December 1985

Ten years after a brief and ill-fated involvement in the civil war that followed the collapse of Portugal's colonial rule, the United States is considering a new attempt to shape the outcome of continuing internal conflict in Angola. The 1976 Clark Amendment prohibiting any military assistance to groups in Angola "unless and until the Congress expressly authorizes such assistance by law" has been repealed by Congress; action is pending on several pieces of legislation that would authorize humanitarian and/or military aid to UNITA; and there is open discussion in Washington (including extensive press coverage) of the possibility of "covert" military assistance carried out under executive branch authority.

Those who view foreign policy issues primarily in globalist East-West terms are tantalized by the notion of a second Angolan venture as a revanchist opportunity to roll back one of the more dramatic projections of Soviet power into the Third World. They also see in Angola an opportunity to act upon an intensified ideological commitment to what they portray as a "revolutionary tradition" of U.S. support for people struggling for democracy.

The case for U.S. intervention is grounded in a set of specific assumptions—that the Soviets and Cubans illegitimately imposed their dominant presence in the country, have perpetuated it by force, and through it threaten the security of neighboring states; and that their dominance might be reversed by means of low-cost, low-risk U.S. assistance to anti-Communist, democratically-inclined insurgents, specifically those of UNITA. Inviting U.S. intervention on the basis of these same assumptions, Savimbi argues that President Reagan's often-expressed desire "to stop Soviet expansionism in the world" can indeed be realized in Angola. American hesitation in the face of such opportunity could mean "handing over all of southern Africa to the Soviet empire."

How justified are the assumptions underlying the proposal to intervene again in Angola? Would military support for Angolan "contras" lead to a reduced Soviet and Cuban presence? Does the choice to be made lie starkly between acceptance of a Soviet fait accompli and assistance to armed insurgents? Or is there a third option?

The Historical Backdrop

The United States seemed relatively unmoved by a "revolutionary tradition" of support for people struggling for democracy during the course of Angola's anticolonial insurgency (1961–1974). In deference to a NATO ally valued for the Azores bases that it contributed to Western defense, a succession of U.S. administrations counseled but did not press strongly for timely Portuguese colonial reform. What modest American succor was extended to Angolan nationalists took the form of a trickle of covert aid to the northern FNLA led by Holden Roberto, an anti-Communist Bakongo émigré based in Zaire.

Unencumbered by ties to colonial authority, the Soviets championed Angolan independence in diplomatic forums throughout the 1960s and early 1970s. They also proselytized and assisted Angolan nationalists, channeling some $60 million of financial, material, and instructional aid through the MPLA. The MPLA's urban, class-oriented, multiracial leadership was notably receptive to Marxist perspectives.

By April 1974, however, when Portuguese military officers weary of more than a decade of fighting insurgency in Guinea-Bissau, Mozambique, and Angola overthrew the authoritarian government of Marcello Caetano in Lisbon, the Soviets had cut back on assistance to the MPLA. The movement had fallen victim to political divisions and its military activities had largely lapsed. Appreciable Soviet assistance resumed only when it became apparent after the Lisbon coup that Chinese and Zairian support for the relatively larger, battle-prone forces of the FNLA might result in the annihilation of a long-term Soviet protégé.

As most of the 350,000 Portuguese residents fled and the Portuguese army faded, Western powers failed to intercede in support of an uneasy coalition (MPLA, FNLA, UNITA) government that the Portuguese, with the blessings of the Organization of African Unity, had established in Luanda. Instead of throwing its weight behind efforts to shore up and promote collaboration within this coalition government, the United States joined the Soviet Union and other external powers in a zero-sum game of fueling frenetic military bids for exclusive political power. The foreign intervention and factional fighting that ensued in 1975 proved so chaotic and opportunistic that its exact sequence may remain forever arguable. Several insights relevant to the policy debate of 1985, however, may be drawn from the confusion.

U.S. policy as much as Soviet audacity assured an outcome that, in the short term, benefited the Soviet Union. Washington's rebuffs to repeated appeals from concerned parties such as Portugal and Zambia for decisive action to save both the coalition government and scheduled elections doomed UNITA's hopes for a strong electoral bid for power. These hopes, never to be tested, were based on its political following within the populous (30 to 40 percent of Angola's approximately 7 million people) Ovimbundu community.

By deciding instead to choose sides and channel covert support through Zaire to the FNLA, the movement most reliant on a military as distinct from a political strategy, Washington helped to insure that the competition for political power in Angola would be decided militarily.

The Soviet Union (and Cuba, a more consistent supporter of the MPLA since the mid-1960s) responded by markedly increasing assistance to the MPLA. The latter, in turn, countered FNLA military occupation of northern Angola by imposing its own military rule over Luanda and its Mbundu hinterland, the traditional center of MPLA political support. UNITA, with the least developed army, tried to stave off its eclipse by turning to South Africa. In so doing, it unwittingly provided the Soviets and Cubans with an internationally acceptable rationale for massive intervention. As evidence of secretive intervention by mobile units from South Africa surfaced in November 1975, potentially strong OAU and other international opposition to the simultaneous arrival of a Soviet-supplied Cuban expeditionary force crumbled.

Upon meeting the first units of Cuban combat troops near Luanda, an FNLA army column of several thousand troops assisted by a South African artillery unit also crumbled, and then fell back chaotically toward the Zairian border leaving abandoned U.S. military equipment strewn across the countryside. A U.S. Congress, wary of post-Vietnam adventures, voted to cut off further funding for covert operations in Angola—operations that by mid-1975 included assistance for UNITA. The South African Defense Force (SADF), which had earlier provided air and logistical support to Portuguese forces (1968–1974), entered the civil war in support of UNITA (and, to a lesser extent, the FNLA) in 1975—with the full encouragement, its leaders intimated, of U.S. Secretary of State Henry Kissinger.

But South Africa was not prepared to confront Soviet and Cuban military power alone. When it became clear that Washington would not or could not provide the backup Pretoria felt had been implicitly pledged, SADF forces with-

drew southward into Namibia, and UNITA guerrillas retreated into the vast forest and savannah of Angola's
southeast. The MPLA proclaimed a People's Republic of
Angola (PRA), embarked upon the creation of a socialist
state, and requested that Cuban forces (now swollen to
some 25,000) remain in order to assure the authority and
security of that state from renewed military assault.

With a startling projection of air and sea power, the
Soviets, prodded by their Cuban allies, had saved their
longtime MPLA beneficiaries from near-certain extinction.
They did so by capitalizing opportunistically on the impro-
vidence of others, including the United States. The result
was a politically privileged presence in Angola that, in
the eyes of most of the world, was regrettable but not
illegitimate.

Limits on Soviet/Cuban Leverage

According to PRA officials, a phased withdrawal of Cuban
forces began as early as April 1976 and their numbers declined by over a third in the following months. The withdrawal was halted and reversed, however, as overflights by
South African aircraft and guerrilla raids by UNITA military units, partly reconstructed and retrained at SADF facilities in Namibia, signaled a new threat.

As it materialized over time, this threat took the form
of (1) SADF attacks on logistical bases and supply lines
of insurgent South West Africa People's Organization
(SWAPO) forces operating from Angola into South African-
held Namibia, attacks that laid waste to a broad swath of
southern Angola; and (2) extension northward of the range
and scope of UNITA insurgency financed at a level of $60
million to $70 million annually (notably by Saudi Arabian
and other Gulf sources), enhanced by Moroccan military
training and supplied through South Africa. Despite increasingly successful efforts to build up its own armed
forces, the PRA became even more dependent on Soviet

arms and Cuban soldiers. The ranks of the latter (including technicians) rose as high as 30,000 at times of maximum pressure from UNITA and South Africa.

To what extent does this dependency also derive from a dominant presence of Soviet and Cuban "advisors" and technicians who prevent the Luanda government from negotiating settlements with its adversaries? Under a policy of "national reconciliation" inaugurated by the PRA's founding president, Agostinho Neto, a considerable number of former adversaries, notably ex-officials of the FNLA, have been brought into the government. And though the Soviet Union's and Cuba's counsel is valued and their role in military and security affairs (along with that of East Germany) is of potentially decisive political importance, they do not have their way on all matters. When one of Moscow's more avid supporters, Nito Alves, attempted a coup in 1977, the Soviet and Cuban ambassadors were sent packing because they had failed to give warning. The Luanda government has seized opportunities to reach border pacification agreements with Zaire and even South Africa without apparent hindrance from its Communist benefactors. Shortly before he was felled by cancer in 1979, President Neto engaged in promising diplomatic conversations with the United States aimed at coupling an expanded program of internal political reconciliation with long-awaited U.S. diplomatic recognition. His death dealt the cause of peace a harsh blow.

The contrastingly "hard line" of some MPLA leaders, notably those scarred by the bitter exile years (1960–1974) marked by perceived American hostility, may be externally encouraged but is not externally imposed. MPLA senior leadership includes persons whose Marxist persuasion, Soviet mentoring, and experience of anticolonial insurgency have rendered them enthusiastic partisans of "scientific socialism." But even they have not blocked the development of mutually advantageous economic ties with Western oil companies, banks, and manufacturers.

In sum, it is the persistence of a serious internal (UNITA) and external (South Africa) armed threat that assures the Soviet Union and Cuba a continuation of their militarily-forged influence in Angola. In the words of PRA President José Eduardo dos Santos, the government does not have the "organized manpower with the required educational level, or the available material and financial resources to wage a war against UNITA . . . and simultaneously to replace Cuban troops and armaments at strategic points in the south, center, and north of the country." To agree to a precipitous departure of Cuban forces, he argues, would be "suicidal."

Relations with Neighboring States

As an avowedly Marxist-Leninist state dependent on the military support of ideologically kindred powers, does the PRA threaten the security of and provoke conflict with neighboring states? Have its Soviet-supported counterinsurgency efforts to pulverize, marginalize, and fragment UNITA spilled across its boundaries?

It is an open secret that UNITA (with or without Kinshasa's assent) has been using Zairian territory to supply its forces in eastern Angola (especially the Cazombo salient lost to the government in September 1985). UNITA also exercises de facto control over border access regions of western Zambia. Most important, it receives major support through adjacent Namibia. UNITA's administrative center of Jamba is situated just north (25 miles by some reports) of the Caprivi Strip. Journalists who fly from Windhoek or other South African airfields to UNITA's military supply base at Licua, then travel another five hours of rough-track road to Jamba, may have the impression of going deep into Angola. They are actually returning toward Caprivi from where UNITA receives, among other things, all the fuel that keeps its fleet of 200 to 300 trucks and its power plants operating. This assistance is freely acknowledged by UNITA. Nevertheless, Angola has limited its reactions to diplomatic demarches in the cases of Zaire and Zambia and to public denunciations of South Africa. No Angolan (let alone Soviet) aircraft have attempted to retaliate against South African facilities used to supply UNITA's military.

The PRA does, however, make its territory available to SWAPO insurgents. Though the UN General Assembly "terminated" South Africa's mandate over Namibia in 1966 and the International Court of Justice has held its continued occupation of the territory to be "illegal," South Africa has evaded international pressure as formulated in Security Council Resolution 435 (1978) to withdraw its army and agree to externally monitored elections leading to independence. Accordingly, the Angolan government cites South African stonewalling, exemplified by the mid-1985 decision to grant internal autonomy to an anti-SWAPO government of its own fashioning, as justification for continued support for the Namibian nationalists.

For its part, the South African government promises to continue to retaliate swiftly against all SWAPO incursions into Namibia and blames Angola for the failure of U.S. diplomatic efforts to produce a Namibian settlement. If the MPLA would only negotiate the entry of Jonas Savimbi and UNITA into the Luanda government, Pretoria argues, Cuban troops, no longer needed, could depart and the way would be open to internationally supervised elections and independence as demanded by the United Nations, the OAU, and SWAPO. From Luanda's perspective, it is South African assistance alone that enables UNITA to pursue its insurgency. Thus, to bring UNITA into the government would be to capitulate to South Africa.

It may not have escaped South Africa's notice that in the process of nourishing a UNITA insurgency that prolongs a Cuban presence that, in turn, preoccupies the United States, it diverts attention away from Namibia (and its own internal "state of emergency"). Expanded UNITA insurgency also serves to divert much of SWAPO's guerrilla army into combat alongside PRA forces.

Although Soviet air and naval craft that reconnoiter the South Atlantic from Angolan facilities made available under terms of the 1976 Soviet-Angolan "Treaty of Friendship and Cooperation" have not violated South African air or sea space, Pretoria's publicists capture U.S. attention by depicting them as threatening. And though Luanda has proposed phased, multiyear withdrawal of Cuban forces in return for implementation of Security Council Resolution 435 in Namibia, South Africa counters with the assertion that nothing less than total, rapid withdrawal will satisfactorily reduce the threat to South African security.

If, in fact, it is not South Africa's dual policy of support for UNITA insurgency and resistance to an internationally-sanctioned settlement in Namibia that creates the need and rationale for an intimidating Soviet and Cuban presence in Angola, there is an obvious way to demonstrate this. It is for South Africa to accept the U.S. diplomatic lead in negotiations with Angola. It is for South Africa to agree that if U.S. negotiators are able to extract what they judge to be a reasonable timetable for a phased withdrawal of most Cuban forces, South Africa will accept the constraints of a good neighbor policy and Security Council Resolution 435 (or a mutually agreed upon equivalent).

Soviet/Cuban Motives and Behavior

That the United States is still brooding over its 1975 humiliation in Angola is evidenced by its lonely, persistent refusal "to reward" Soviet and Cuban expansionism by recognizing and establishing diplomatic relations with the PRA. A punitive, "get even" mindset encourages the notion that the Soviets can be made to pay dearly for their Angolan advantage and that such a cost-benefit shift will ultimately cause them to give in and leave.

Several probabilities concerning Soviet motives and behavior argue against such reasoning. Having failed to provide the Marxist-Leninist government of Mozambique with either the economic or military wherewithal to secure its authority in the face of a partially self-inflicted economic disaster, a devastating drought, and a South African-supported antigovernment insurgency, the Soviet Union suffered a severe political embarrassment in 1984. In March of that year, Mozambique "sued for peace" and signed the Nkomati agreement with South Africa. Under the terms of that accord, Mozambique cut off assistance to the would-be insurgent African National Congress (ANC) of South Africa. It also opened its doors to economic and technological relations with South Africa and Western countries.

Sensitive to this blow, a rejuvenated Soviet leadership under Mikhail Gorbachev should not be expected to tolerate a dramatic, "under the gun" reversal in Angola, where the Soviets (along with Cuba) have far more at stake than was the case in Mozambique. Indeed, the increased magnitude and effectiveness of the Soviet military role as evidenced in sophisticated equipment and reported behind-the-lines command roles during the Angolan government's August-September 1985 offensive against UNITA strongholds reflect long-term planning and commitment.

Presumably as determined as his predecessors to assert the Soviet Union's status as a fully global power, Gorbachev may be expected to strive for selective Third World successes. At the very least, he will need to phase, delimit, and rationalize any losses. In Angola that would include stressing South African concessions (Namibia) while dissimulating his own (Cuban withdrawals). Put another way, it would be unproductive for the United States to try to force a Soviet leader into the humiliation of being perceived as having "lost" Angola to South African-backed insurgents.

Might U.S.-assisted escalation of UNITA insurgency, however, raise the cost to Moscow of Soviet and Cuban intervention to an intolerable level? In fact, it is Angola, not the Soviet Union, which pays the devastating human and material price of continuing war. Angolan pays for the Soviet weaponry, the MiG-21s and -23s, the Mi-24 helicopter gunships, the tanks, trucks, and artillery. It uses upward from 50 percent of its oil revenues of over $2 billion annually to purchase Soviet arms and to maintain Cuban troops and technicians (25,000 to 30,000). The resources thus diverted from the urgent needs of reconstruction and development provide the Soviets with significant arms sales which they would not be discommoded to increase. Herein lies a Soviet-Angolan conflict of interests that U.S. diplomacy should indeed exploit by helping the Angolans find an "honorable" way out of the cycle of endless, resource-consuming violence.

Gains and Risks of U.S. Intervention

For the Soviets and Cubans, the benefits of remaining (prestige, arms sales, ideological impact, regional presence, limitation of Western influence) outweigh the costs (modest Cuban casualties, damage to U.S.-Soviet relations, Angolan resentment of dependency). What might be the gains and losses or risks for the United States should it join UNITA/ South African efforts to alter the Soviet/Cuban cost-benefit ratio and force the MPLA government to its knees? They would likely be simultaneously economic, diplomatic, political, and military.

Economic. U.S. oil companies in partnership with Angola's state oil corporation, SONANGOL, are exploring and pumping from what are estimated to be reserves of 1.7 billion barrels of high-grade petroleum. Chevron (Cabinda Gulf), Texaco, and Conoco, along with Elf Aquitaine of France and other Western firms, have invested millions of dollars in profitable operations. American private banks, such as Chase Manhattan, and the U.S. Export-Import Bank have together lent in the neighborhood of half a billion dollars. Boeing, General Tire, and other U.S. companies have profitably joined in investing in Angola and selling to the tough-bargaining MPLA government, which all of them praise for honesty, reliability, and pragmatism. The United States has become Angola's number one trading partner with annual two-way trade totaling over $1 billion.

To put this economic involvement in jeopardy and to

boycott the products of Chevron or other investors in Angola, as some conservative zealots propose, would be to signal to the world that U.S. enterprise may become hostage to erratic fluctuations in American politics. The result could be to disadvantage American business in its competition with Western Europeans, the Japanese, and others, who would be only too happy, for example, to assume a larger role in Angola's oil production, or to replace "unreliable" U.S. enterprise elsewhere. Nor should the potential damage to American lenders to Angola, vulnerable to retaliation and heavy losses, be underestimated.

The opportunity costs of an Angolan adventure would assuredly include the loss of ideological or political spinoffs that might otherwise be anticipated from Angola's steadily increasing reliance on U.S. capital and technology. Even confirmed Luanda Marxists have come to respect American know-how and business practices.

American economic influence may not offer the instant gratification of a battlefield victory, but it does offer grounds for optimism on the part of those who would change Angola by example rather than by force. For instance, a Louisiana sugar company has been hired to run an aging sugarcane mill, replacing Cuban technicians unable to operate it effectively. Arthur D. Little serves as a financial consultant to the Angolan government and runs training courses for its technocrats.

Only able or willing to deliver in the military field, the Soviets would be cheered by a Washington policy shift that undercut the United States' growing economic influence. It is this penetrating influence that renders plausible Western hopes that a young, emerging technocratic elite exposed to Western values and practices may gradually gain ascendancy over doctrinaire party veterans and bring about political liberalization. A predictably unifying, rigidifying reaction to an American decision to join South Africa in support of antigovernment insurgency, however, could severely damage these hopes.

Diplomatic. Diplomatic costs would derive from perceptions that the United States had entered into an alliance with South Africa. It is virtually impossible to determine to what extent UNITA's military successes of recent years are due to UNITA's own or South African prowess. The South African commando team apprehended while moving in to sabotage U.S. oil installations in Cabinda in May 1985 was carrying UNITA leaflets which, according to the unit's captured commander, were to be left behind. This incident raised questions about who may have been responsible for earlier sabotage of railroads, power pylons, dams, and factories previously ascribed to and claimed by UNITA. Indeed, UNITA may have been responsible. But the pervasive secrecy and dissimulation that have surrounded UNITA's relations with South Africa since 1975 have made it impossible to distinguish clearly between the actions of the two parties. Protest as UNITA must that Angolan issues should be viewed totally apart from those of South Africa, whose racial practices it deplores, UNITA's image has become merged with the country whose patronage it finds at once an enormous asset and a liability.

Is the United States to become caught up in this same kind of association? Western European economic interests might welcome the competitive advantage that would befall them in the event of such an American predicament. But the governments of Western Europe should be expected to respond with anxiety to such perceived impetuosity. American leadership in the Western community depends in great measure on confidence in U.S. judgment, on an understanding that Americans will use force only as a last resort.

At their 1985 annual summit meeting, African heads of state declared that any U.S. financial, logistical, or military support for UNITA, private or public, direct or through third parties, would constitute a "hostile act against the Organization of African Unity." But it is not only European allies and African states whose confidence in Washington's sense and purpose would be shaken. A major U.S. plunge into the Angolan conflict (and it would have to be major to have any hope of success) would risk damage to the United States' stature in the world at large.

Political. Under pressure from local and state governments, churches, labor, students, businesses – a broad spectrum of U.S. institutions – the U.S. government has been endeavoring to distance itself from association with the apartheid system of South Africa. Intensified racial violence and repression in that country reported in galvanizing detail by the American press and displayed vividly on television has rendered apartheid a household word. Black Americans, in particular, have been motivated to mobilize in TransAfrica and the Free South Africa Movement the politically potent foreign policy lobby long expected of them.

For the U.S. government to choose this time to ally itself with South Africa would be gratuitously to invite racial discord. It would endanger domestic peace and diminish the country's collective sense of self-respect. The damage to the U.S. polity could be enormous.

Military. Might an infusion of U.S. finance and weaponry enable UNITA to hold its fixed bases in Cuando Cubango province in the southeast against future government offensives? Though UNITA denies it, most battle reportage suggests that it took direct South African participation to turn back the August-September 1985 assault on UNITA's strongholds. Required, according to these reports, was intervention by the 32 Battalion (crack "foreign legion" troops, mostly ex-FNLA), the South African air force (principally night raids), and heavy artillery (against Soviet tanks).

Pretoria also felt a need to reassure Savimbi publicly that he would not be abandoned. At the time of the battle for Mavinga, South African political and military leaders issued their first official acknowledgment of longtime assistance and warned that they would not sit by and allow UNITA to be crushed. Simultaneously, they brought pressure on Washington to join in stemming the advance of

allegedly Soviet-directed PRA forces toward the Caprivi/
Namibia border.

The PRA sees extension of the range of its air power
(some 80 percent of which is reportedly piloted by Angolans, up from 40 percent three years ago) as the key to
future success. The dos Santos government has set as a top
priority the southeastward extension of military communications and infrastructure, including the forward placement
of mobile radar units. For the time being, Angolan air force
commander Colonel Iko Carreira acknowledges, the South
Africans enjoy a tactical advantage in southeast Angola
because of "ultramodern" bases in the Caprivi Strip. The
nearest Angolan air base is at Menongue, about 500 kilometers from Jamba. South African aircraft are able to intervene rapidly and to time their actions so as to catch Angolan aircraft just as they prepare to return to base. "The
reinforcement of our air force," Carreira is quoted as saying
in the October 21, 1985 issue of *Afrique-Asie*, is "essential."

The Soviets will presumably work with the PRA during
the December–April rainy season to prepare for this extension of air power. It seems probable, therefore, that the next
battle for Mavinga and Jamba will require greater air protection for UNITA ground forces. The alternative is for
UNITA to abandon conventional, fixed-position warfare
and return to guerrilla-style insurgency.

Will the South African air force take on MiG-21s and
-23s with its own aging and (because of the international
arms embargo against Pretoria) largely irreplaceable Impal-
as and Mirage F-1s? Or will the United States, as the October 30, 1985 issue of *Africa Confidential* acidly suggests,
provide air defense systems that might or might not prove
sufficient "to preserve Jamba, complete with candelabras
and butlers?" The risk is that an involved United States
could find itself, as in 1975, confronted with a crisis choice of
either providing massive support to besieged UNITA and
South African forces or accepting a humiliating retreat.

The military realities of Angola will not be altered by a
few tens of millions of dollars, let alone "humanitarian" aid.

In response to the challenge it faces, the PRA has expanded its armed forces to some 75,000 men (excluding foreign personnel that include, in addition to some 30,000 Cubans, up to 3,000 Eastern bloc and Yugoslav advisors and technicians). Portuguese counterinsurgency specialists have helped to improve the combat effectiveness of PRA ground forces. Soviet and Yugoslav arms deliveries have risen.

There has reportedly been much wastage of equipment due to Soviet efforts to impose a costly European technology and style of warfare on a Third World state. Nonetheless, the military sector is the Soviet Union's strong card. If the United States chooses to play to it, Washington must be prepared to pay a heavy price for success. Prospects for an intensified offensive against UNITA and even a direct clash between Angolan and South African forces will mount with the end of the rainy season in April 1986. What price the United States might have to pay to determine the outcome of such encounters seems unclear but daunting.

Were UNITA to give up its pretensions to being a state within a state, however, it might avoid a crushing showdown. It could redeploy its 15,000 to 20,000 soldiers (plus a like number of local militia) into diffused, shifting, unconventional guerrilla units against which air power and tanks would be relatively ineffective. By encouraging UNITA to parade the fixed trappings of statehood before the world press, however, UNITA's external backers may be rendering it more susceptible to annihilation by the bombers, helicopters, tanks, and missiles provided by the Soviet Union. Should U.S. assistance further encourage this propensity for high-stakes conventional warfare, it might also unintentionally contribute to UNITA's demise.

Why Ideology Is Not the Issue

As a movement fighting for democracy, does UNITA not deserve U.S. support as a matter of basic principle, whatever the odds or cost? Even its enemies grant that UNITA enjoys a following among the rural populace of central Angola, among traditional chiefs (*sobas*), among Protestants alienated by the government's heavy-handed antireligious bias ("believers" may not be members of the MPLA), and among some dislocated and impoverished towndwellers. And it may be argued that those of UNITA's leadership, including Savimbi, who were educated in missionary schools and were to some extent socialized into the nonhierarchical collegiality of American Congregational and United Church of Canada Protestantism acquired a lasting commitment to democratic values. It is even sometimes suggested that a traditional stress on consensus decision making within Ovimbundu culture predisposes some top UNITA leadership to value democratic process.

UNITA, on the other hand, is firmly led by one internally and externally lionized man. As an insurgent movement engaged in a merciless civil war, it can scarcely be expected to function democratically. And there are persistent reports of dissension within its ranks about Savimbi's leadership (given credibility by the recent defection of a ranking Ovambo leader, António Vakulukuta) and ethnic dissidence on the part of Chokwes and other non-Ovimbundu. Relevant to all this, Harvard political scientist Samuel P. Huntington observed in the *Political Science Quarterly* (Summer 1984) that while "all revolutionary opponents of authoritarian regimes claim to be democratic," once they achieve power "almost all turn out to be authoritarian." "Guerrilla insurgencies," he concludes, "do not inaugurate democratic regimes."

Given the enthusiasm of American conservatives and neoconservatives, it might be assumed that UNITA is at least an avid backer of free enterprise. Not if the resolutions of UNITA conferences or the logo on its official seal are to be believed. The logo reads: "Socialism, Negritude, Democracy, Nonalignment." This is not to argue that UNITA's ranks do not include persons committed to pragmatic economics. MPLA ranks also include such persons, however. Ideological professions and strategic alliances aside and the war over, either the MPLA or UNITA in power might be expected to adopt essentially pragmatic, nationalist policies and to govern in an initially largely authoritarian manner. There would be differences. But the choice is not between good and evil, democratic and totalitarian.

The Case for Prudence

Though there may be special circumstances in which U.S. assistance to antigovernment insurgents can be justified, it should never become a cathartic substitute for patient and imaginative diplomacy. It should never be seen as a substitute for or become a block to instructive and constructive economic and cultural relations in serving the enlightened long-term interests of the United States.

In Africa, as the Defense Department's Noel C. Koch has observed, the Soviets have generally behaved so badly that the "last residue" of their influence may well disappear by the end of this century without our having to do much of anything. He cites their behavior in Angola as a case in point. The Soviets sell expensive, complicated military equipment to Angola but do not provide adequate training for its maintenance. This leaves Angolans dependent on the continuing presence of a large number of Soviet and East bloc technicians. The Soviets also profit exorbitantly from a fishing agreement under which they have again provided little training for Angolans and under which their trawlers vacuum Angolan waters of fish, "scrape the seabed and take everything on which fish and seafood depend to survive and regenerate themselves."

Angolans are not unobservant, nor are they immune to yearnings for peace after a quarter century of war. Though it may be frustratingly slow, it is steady, insistent, reasoned diplomacy aimed at encouraging negotiated, noncoercive solutions to internal and cross-boundary conflict and not military intervention that still represents the most promising and prudent course for U.S. policy. Angola poses a test of our maturity. The United States should face this test with confidence in the persuasive power of its economic, cultural, and political example.

4

The Angolan Economy: A Status Report

Gillian Gunn

May 1986

In common with other oil-exporting countries, Angola has been shaken by the sharp oil price fall that began in December 1985. The revenue drop is straining an economy already overstretched by a quarter century of war and a decade of overcentralization since independence in 1975. But even taking into account the new possibility of de facto economic sanctions by its major trading partner (the United States), Angola's outlook is not as grim as that of many other Third World states. Among the reasons for its resilience are the following:

- a significant amount of bureaucratic, travel, and personal remittance spending is being cut with relatively little pain;
- Angola enjoys a good credit rating and international banks regard payment delay requests sympathetically;
- several post-1980 oil investments are beginning to bear fruit and rising production is partially compensating for the price fall;
- measures to decentralize the economy and offer more material incentives introduced at the Second Congress of the ruling MPLA in December 1985 may provide modest economic impetus, even though implementation will be hampered by the war;

- while the prospect that the United States might cut credit, restrict U.S. exports, and force corporate disinvestment concerns the MPLA government, there is an impressive line of European banks, exporters, and investors willing and able to fill any vacancy.

Riding Out the Oil Glut

Angolan statistics are notoriously hard to pin down, but it is clear that petroleum provides approximately 90 percent of the country's total foreign exchange earnings, which have averaged between $1.5 and $2 billion per year for the last three years. The 1986 budget was drafted on the assumption that oil prices would remain at about $25 per barrel. The price began to slip in December 1985, and when it hit $18 a barrel on February 4, 1986, President José Eduardo dos Santos estimated a loss of $600 million in 1986 earnings, about a third of the budget, even without any further price decline. The price eventually dropped to below $10 a barrel, though it has since partially recovered.

Oil production, which rose from 130,000 barrels per day (b/d) in the late 1970s to an estimated 285,000 b/d at the end of 1985, had been expected to continue its upward spiral this year, putting Angola on target for its goal of 500,000 b/d in 1990. Unlike some other non-OPEC oil producers, however, Angola is taking the long view, seeking to strike a balance between the need to raise production now to increase revenue and the desirability of keeping the oil in the ground while the price is poor. Production will probably grow only moderately this year, but will still reach at least 300,000 b/d. Taking account of local consumption needs, this will earn between one-half and two-thirds of last year's revenue, depending upon price fluctuations.

Oil company interest does not seem to have waned. Total investment, by both the state oil company SONANGOL and foreign firms, is slated to increase 46 percent in 1986. Six of the 13 offshore "blocks" opened for exploration in

1978 have been taken up, and a seventh is in negotiation. The foreign companies now operating in Angola include Chevron, Conoco, Petrofina, Texaco, Elf Aquitaine, Agip, British Petroleum, Braspetro, Total, Cities Services, Mitsubishi, and Marathon. The only company to pull out recently was Mobil, and there was stiff competition to buy up its 25 percent share in Block 3, with Mitsubishi the eventual purchaser. Almost simultaneously, Conoco concluded a new contract to become the operating company in Block 5. In February 1986, the president of Chevron Overseas Petroleum personally reassured President dos Santos of Chevron's readiness to continue expanding its oil operation. A month earlier Elf's chairman had told dos Santos that "we think Angola will be one of the most important sites for our group."

There are four reasons for Angola's popularity with the oil industry. First, the "production cost" of Angolan oil is said to be relatively low, so healthy profits are possible despite present depressed prices. Second, offshore Angolan oil deposits are especially rich. There are an estimated 1.84 billion barrels of proven reserves, and new finds occur regularly. Third, Angolan oil is of good quality, with a fairly low sulfur content, and is relatively easy to refine. Finally, the oil industry views Angola as a reliable partner. Once a contract is signed, Luanda lives up to it. Indeed, one veteran oil executive recently named Angola as his favorite country in which to operate: "When you come to the Angolans with a problem, their first instinct is how can they help you, not how can they cause more difficulties."

The Costs of War

As John Marcum recounts in earlier chapters of this volume, Angola has actually fought two wars over the past 25 years. The first began in 1961, when nationalist groups initiated guerrilla operations against Portuguese colonial rule, and continued until 1974, when the Portuguese regime was overthrown in a coup engineered by a military weary of Lisbon's several African colonial wars. Some 300,000 Portuguese departed when Angola became independent in 1975, taking much vital equipment with them and sabotaging what they left behind. It is estimated that over three-quarters of the country's vehicles were removed, and 6,250 Portuguese-operated commercial farms were abandoned. Because Portuguese educational policy had not encouraged the development of African managerial skills, those aspects of the economy which remained functional in the wake of independence were often mismanaged.

Even before formal independence, the prospects of economic recovery had been further dimmed by the onset of Angola's second war—a civil struggle pitting the new MPLA government in Luanda against two other movements with which the MPLA had been allied in the common rebellion against Portuguese domination.

Armed clashes between the MPLA and Holden Roberto's FNLA virtually destroyed the rich coffee plantations in the northeast which had supplied a fifth of the world's robusta imports. Angolan coffee production plummeted by 80 percent from 1974 to 1981. By 1976, the FNLA's ability to pose a serious threat had ended, and by 1984 a large portion of the FNLA leadership had been integrated into the MPLA.

Jonas Savimbi's UNITA proved to be a more enduring threat, increasingly disrupting the southern third of the country. The vital Benguela railroad, designed to carry Zambian, Zairian, and Angolan exports from the interior to the coast, has been largely nonoperational since 1975. In 1984, the railroad carried one-tenth of its preindependence traffic, and this only along a relatively short stretch between Huambo and the coast.

The formerly lucrative diamond industry has also been damaged by repeated UNITA attacks. One recent incident, in March 1986, involved the kidnapping of over 150 foreign workers from the northeastern mining town of Andrada. In 1985 the mining company DIAMANG, 77 percent owned by the Angolan state, fulfilled less than two-thirds of its production plan, and replaced Britain's Mining and Technical Services company (MATS), which was helping run the operation, with another firm. Production as of 1986 is estimated at below a third of the preindependence level.

Smuggling has also cut deeply into diamond income. A major diamond trading operation has blossomed in Lisbon in the last few years, apparently fueled by diamonds exported illegally from Angola. Initially, many of the stones came through the "kamanga" network of Angolan airline pilots and local businessmen. Although this ring was broken in 1984, the stones are still flowing to Lisbon through other channels. Diamond industry experts believe UNITA may be directly supplying the market, and Savimbi himself has stated that diamond sales pay for some of his war costs. There are reports that more than a dozen "diamond stores" have been established along the Angola-Zaire border. In May 1986 Luanda accused units of the South African Defense Force allegedly occupying Cuando Cubango province of "negotiating illegally the selling of timber, skins, and diamonds" in cooperation with "UNITA bandits."

Ironically, South Africa is also involved in the legal diamond trade. The De Beers Central Selling Organization has long held the contract for marketing DIAMANG's production, and reportedly has a good working relationship with the MPLA. This is virtually the only known commercial economic link between South Africa and Luanda that survived independence and the departure of the Portuguese.

Independent reports now seem to support MPLA allegations of South African complicity in the illicit timber trade. On May 4, 1986, *The Observer* (London) quoted the claim of a Portuguese businessman in Johannesburg that he buys thousands of tons of "valuable teak and other tropical hardwoods" that are felled by UNITA soldiers and floated down the Cuando river out of southern Angola to an assembly point in Namibia's Caprivi Strip.

Iron ore was in earlier times Angola's fourth most important export. Production at the Cassinga mine in the south halted in 1975. An Austrian firm undertook to rehabilitate the complex in 1984, and hoped to begin production at the end of 1985, but repeated raids on the mine and on the railway linking it to the port at Namibe have slowed the operation.

The war's most serious impact, however, has been in the agricultural sector. Production in some parts of the country, already hampered by inappropriate government policies, is further impeded by the planting of land mines by UNITA guerrillas. Crops rotting in fields is a not uncommon sight, as farmers in some areas are afraid to venture out for harvest. Sabotage of transport routes has interrupted the movement of produce from the rural areas to the cities. As a result of this combination of factors, the state markets in Luanda are empty. Although food is available in the "candonga" black markets, it is extremely expensive. Indeed, one such market has been nicknamed "Tira Bikini" ("Underwear Strip"), presumably because one figuratively has to sell even one's underwear in order to pay the high prices.

At a May 15 (1986) meeting of aid donors in Luanda, the government reported that "about 600,000 people [were] suffering from hunger, diseases of undernourishment, and other ills . . . ," especially in central areas of the country. Although Angola was affected by southern Africa's recent drought, UNDP, UNICEF, and Red Cross officials working in the area say the war is responsible for most of the suffering. The agricultural disruption has reportedly required Angola to import about 80 percent of its food in recent years, at a cost of $250–$300 million per year.

There have been some South African and/or UNITA operations against the oil sector. A South African commando unit unsuccessfully attacked the oil storage depots at Chevron's Cabinda operation in May 1985. The captured

leader, Captain Wynand du Toit, subsequently explained at
a lengthy Luanda press conference which this writer attended that the unit had intended to leave UNITA litera-
ture on the site, thus permitting the guerrillas to take credit
for the raid and covering up Pretoria's role. In March 1986,
UNITA claimed to have hit an oil pipeline in Cabinda, and
in early April announced it had sabotaged the province's
water and electricity supply. Both claims were denied by
the MPLA and Chevron.

Yet another economic cost of the war is the requirement
to divert resources that are badly needed to rebuild the
productive sector. Though no firm figures are available, experts estimate that between 30 and 50 percent of Angola's
foreign exchange earnings go to war-related expenditures.
With the drop in oil prices the percentage will now probably
rise. (Western diplomats believe that Cuba has received foreign exchange compensation for the services of the Cuban
troops [currently 30,000–35,000] present in the country at
Luanda's request since independence, but the MPLA has
not confirmed this. Angola reportedly ceased paying
Havana for Cuban nonmilitary personnel in late 1984, but it
is not clear if the presumed military payments were similarly forgiven.)

Although the war is exacting a heavy economic price,
the situation is not comparable to that in Mozambique. In
Angola, geographic factors provide the major revenue-earn-
ing sector with unique insulation from a guerrilla siege. The
most important oil operations are isolated in the northern
Cabinda province, a coastal enclave at the opposite end of
the country from UNITA's southern stronghold. To reach
Cabinda, UNITA forces would have to come through the
neighboring state of Congo (an MPLA ally) or cross the
narrow strip of Zairian territory that separates the enclave
from the rest of Angola. In 1978 Zaire's President Mobuto
Sese Seko made an agreement with the late President Agostinho Neto promising to prevent such infiltrations, and in
February 1985 he and President dos Santos agreed to establish a joint commission to ensure that neither country's

territory would be used as a base for "subversive groups." Although the MPLA doubts Mobutu is living up to the letter of the deal, the accord does provide some protection. Most of the oil operations are offshore, and the onshore installations are concentrated in a small area, well guarded by Angolan troops. Cuban troops based in Cabinda province provide additional security.

The U.S. Enigma

Until late 1985, the Reagan administration, like the Carter administration before it, took a neutral or even encouraging position with regard to the activities of U.S. corporations in Angola. Indeed, oil company executives say that the relevant departments of the U.S. government applauded their operations in Angola as a legitimate contribution to the regional dimension of "constructive engagement." In late January 1986, however, Assistant Secretary of State for African Affairs Chester Crocker, in a statement that raised more questions than it answered, said that Chevron and other companies operating in Angola "should be thinking about U.S. national interests as well as their own corporate interests as they make their decisions." State Department deputy spokesman Charles Redman was more explicit in a March 25 press briefing. "U.S. economic policy toward Angola," he said, "is (1) to deny, pending an achievement of a negotiated settlement, all U.S. exports to Angola with a military use, and (2) to not support Angola's ability to earn foreign currency and thus fund its war against UNITA until the government of Angola demonstrates clear intent to reach a negotiated settlement on Namibian independence and in that context Cuban troop withdrawal."

In accordance with these new policy guidelines, the planned purchase by Angola of a Lockheed LC-100, a commercial version of the Hercules, was recently blocked when the Department of Commerce denied a license on the grounds that such an aircraft could conceivably be used to transport Cuban military personnel. Angola's national airline, TAAG, would like to buy three new Boeing 737s for its commercial operations, but is hesitant to place the order for fear of another license denial.

U.S. Export-Import Bank export credit support for sales to Angola is also under threat. In the last quarter of 1985, Exim reportedly was required to adopt a new policy of refusing to finance any sale that would provide major revenues to the MPLA or assist the war effort. This could be interpreted to rule out everything except food exports. Legislation has been proposed in Congress that would formalize and possibly expand existing restrictions on Exim finance for Angola. As of the end of April 1986, Exim's exposure in Angola amounted to $202 million, down from $242 million at the end of 1984.

Some experts on export finance contend that even a total suspension of Exim facilities for Angola would probably not hurt Luanda as much as it would hurt a range of U.S. interests. Angola's payment record places it in the good graces of the European export credit agencies, such as France's Coface and Britain's ECGD. The European Airbus consortium is waiting to leap in should the Boeing sale fall through. In addition, Angola's 1985 decision to join the Lomé Convention, the vehicle through which EEC aid is channeled to the Third World, means European firms may be able to plug into this source to finance their sales. An EEC delegation visited Angola in March 1986 and confirmed that the country would receive $95 million in aid over the coming five years. And on May 14, 1986, Angola signed its first general cooperation agreement with Britain; a joint commission will be set up in 1987 to discuss bilateral agreements in specific fields. An investment and trade conference scheduled to take place in Luanda in June 1986 has attracted over 30, mainly European, corporate participants. Thus, if the Exim connection is completely severed, the U.S. aerospace and oil industries may suffer more than the MPLA.

The most high-profile pressure on the U.S. oil industry

is the "Chevron-Gulf Out of Angola" campaign launched in December 1985 by the Conservative Caucus Foundation, a private lobbying group that categorizes UNITA among the world's top "anti-Communist freedom fighters" and favors all-out U.S. moral and military support of the Savimbi movement. Chevron shareholders have been urged to pressure the company to withdraw from Angola; Chevron stations are subject to intermittent boycotts; and the Department of Defense is being pressed to review Chevron's military contracts across the board in light of its continuing operations in a country "allied to the Soviet Union."

This campaign faces several obstacles. Some U.S. officials doubt that under present law an otherwise qualified contractor can be excluded from bidding for government contracts merely because it does business with a country that does not meet a Washington litmus test based on ideology. One possible justification for such exclusion might be the Cuban Assets Control regulations. Congressional sources say even conservative legislators are uneasy about tampering with procurement regulations (i.e. banning Chevron military contracts through new laws). Meanwhile, the Securities and Exchange Commission is reportedly considering "informally" whether the Conservative Caucus Foundation improperly sought shareholder support against Chevron management.

If Chevron were forced out, oil industry sources say France's Elf is only one of several oil companies that have expressed interest in filling the gap. Chevron has just completed a number of investments in Angola, and the resultant revenues are coming on stream now, making the property extremely attractive. If such a deal were struck, Angola would negotiate a new contract with the inheritor of Chevron's assets. One of the many ironies in the anti-Chevron campaign is that the company's Gulf component received particularly good terms from the Portuguese in the agreement negotiated before independence, and these were only partially modified when the MPLA took over. Since

Angola's contract negotiation skills have subsequently improved, any future deal would probably be more favorable to the government than Chevron-Gulf's. Thus, while the MPLA would be inconvenienced by the short-term disruption of a changeover to another company, it might actually get more dollars per barrel in the long run if Chevron pulled out.

Debt Management

Angola's total debt is estimated at a relatively modest $2.7 billion, of which about half is owed to the West. When the oil price started to fall, government officials immediately began conversations with European banks. They were told that short-term commercial debt would continue to be serviced as before, while repayment of medium-term commercial debt would be delayed by about two months. Some export credit agencies were also approached and payment delays, possibly amounting to four or five months, were discussed on a case-by-case basis.

Banking sources report that the financial community responded positively and agreed to be flexible on payment deadlines. Angola apparently wants to avoid a general rescheduling, and the banks now believe such a move will not be necessary. Indeed, banks seem willing not only to accept payment delays for old loans, but also to make new ones. In March 1986, Citibank opened a new line of credit to finance Angola's agricultural, industrial, and oil sectors.

One reason for the bankers' positive response is the prospect that Angola may join the IMF and the World Bank. The government reportedly decided in late 1985 to become a member of both institutions, but in light of increased U.S. hostility has delayed making applications for fear Washington might lobby to block entry.

Angola's debt service ratio in 1985 was about 16 percent. Before the oil price drop it was scheduled to rise to just under 20 percent for 1986. The subsequent decline in foreign exchange revenue means that the ratio probably will now rise to just under 30 percent. Since payment delays were planned on the assumption that interest would be in the 11 percent range, and the rate is now about two points lower, there is some extra breathing space. President dos Santos probably discussed payment delays on Angola's debts to the Soviet Union when he visited Moscow in early May 1986. In this connection, it is noteworthy that the socialist countries agreed to roll over the debt the last time Angola had a payments problem.

The MPLA's Second Congress

The MPLA held its Second Party Congress in early December 1985, just before the oil price fall. The Congress ratified a number of possibly crucial economic reforms, of which the most important was the decentralization of economic management. Whereas previously an enterprise manager had responsibility for results, but day-to-day decisions were often made by a central authority, the Congress ruled that day-to-day decisions should now rest with the local manager. He will receive overall direction from the center at the beginning of the year and must render account at the end of the year, but within those restrictions has freedom of action.

Another important decision had to do with state farms. Though they will not be abandoned, more emphasis will be given to the peasant private and loosely structured cooperative sectors, which produce most of Angola's food. In order to stimulate peasant production, the government plans to send consumer goods out to the rural areas, giving the peasant something to buy with the local currency he receives in payment for his crop.

Among further undertakings to provide incentives, the Congress favorably viewed the possibility of giving some sectors, particularly agriculture and firms producing for export, foreign exchange payments in return for high production.

The Congress also addressed the problem of the over-valued local currency, the kwanza. Currently five small and rather anemic tomatoes purchased on the Luanda "candonga" cost the equivalent of $30 at official exchange rates. Whiskey is becoming a parallel currency, and traders suddenly produce goods not seen on the market for years if a bottle of this commodity is offered. At the Congress, a commitment was made to "create conditions [for] stabilizing the purchasing power of the national currency by establishing rigorous controls over increased amounts of money in circulation and ensuring supplies of goods and services to satisfy the solvent demands of the population, while creating the appropriate mechanisms for fighting . . . black-marketeering." It is not clear if this means devaluation. As of mid-1986, the kwanza trades on the black market for less than a tenth of its official value ($1 = Kz29.918), and Angolan economic experts say that a modest devaluation may occur in the next 12 months.

The Congress also looked at ways to economize. It particularly focused on the cost of those technical advisors compensated in foreign exchange, implicitly targeting the Western technicians, and concluded that a greater effort should be made to find and/or train Angolan replacements. Officials subsequently conceded that education and training facilities must be improved before the full replacement process can be executed, but noted that bureaucratic inertia had hindered use of those young people who have already been trained. The Congress also de-emphasized the creation of big new projects and highlighted the need to concentrate on the completion of existing projects and rehabilitation of installations that had fallen into disrepair.

While the Congress took a negative view toward foreign technical contracts, it was positive about foreign investment. The need to redraft the investment code to make it easier to understand and more attractive to potential investors was discussed, and a new code may be issued in early 1987.

Austerity and Ministerial Changes

Angola's ability to withstand the economic challenges it faces has been bolstered by the speed with which it imposed austerity measures. Even government officials concede that the governing elite was living a little too well before the oil price dropped. There was a lot of unnecessary spending by ministries, particularly on foreign travel. Some Angolans say that the oil price fall "is a blessing in disguise because it is forcing us to correct our spendthrift ways."

Measures to limit foreign exchange expenditures on personal remittances, telex and telephone charges, and foreign travel were implemented within weeks of the oil price crash. Imports have also been drastically cut. Although no official statistics are available, it is evident that every ministry is feeling the pinch. Imports associated with projects that are not likely to bring in immediate foreign exchange earnings or promote import substitution are near the bottom of the priority list. This will delay some important infrastructure development programs.

In addition to imposing austerity measures, Angola has responded to the oil glut by restructuring economic management. In February 1986, dos Santos created three new "minister of state" positions covering the "productive sphere," the "economic and social sphere," and the "sphere of inspection and state control." Energy and Petroleum Minister Pedro de Castro dos Santos Van Dúnem (often referred to as "Loy") received the first and most influential post, while an alternate-member of the MPLA politburo, Maria Mambo Café, received the second. The third post, which is still not well defined but is expected to assist in combating corruption, went to Benguela Provincial Commissioner Kundi Payama. Loy and Mambo Café are responsible for coordinating the activities of the various ministries and secretariats involved in economic decision making. Dos Santos may hope that this rearrangement will make management more efficient than when long-reigning Minister of Planning Lopo do Nascimento controlled the liaison function. Loy is well regarded by the foreign oil executives with whom he has had extensive contact in his role as petroleum minister.

The Longer Run

Angola's current economic difficulties sometimes cause foreign analysts to forget that, in terms of resources, this is one of the richest countries in Africa.

Currently only about 2–3 percent of arable land is cultivated. One aid technician recently lamented the irony that "people are going hungry in a country so fertile that if you drop a seed on the ground and come back six months later, you have food." Angola's diamonds are qualitatively among the best in the world, and reserves are nowhere near depletion. The Benguela railroad could earn considerable foreign exchange if the route were secure. Apart from the iron ore mines, which could be rehabilitated once peace returned to the south, Angola also has reserves of manganese, copper, lead, zinc, and gold which have hardly been touched. New oil is constantly being found, and exploitation has not even begun of the 51 billion cubic meters of natural gas associated with the oil deposits. The Luanda oil refinery currently runs at near capacity and is slated for expansion.

Angola also has major hydroelectric possibilities. Plans to build (with Brazilian and Soviet help) a dam on the Cuanza river at Kapanda, in the northwestern part of the country, are currently moving slowly because of the austerity conditions and occasional security problems. The Ruacaná project in the south, partially constructed as a joint Portuguese-South African enterprise before independence, has long been operating at a low level because of the border war. Angola is responsible for energy matters within the Southern African Development Coordination Conference (SADCC), and has the potential to supply much of the SADCC region if transport routes were secure.

A surprisingly well-developed industrial base is already

in place. A brief tour of the outskirts of Luanda reveals dozens of small factories lying idle because of the shortage of spare parts and raw materials. Before independence these supplied a wide range of consumer goods. An example of the potential vigor of the industrial sector is the recent rehabilitation of the CIMANGOLA cement plant in Luanda with Danish assistance. Cement exports, halted in 1980, are due to resume this year and should eventually earn Angola significant foreign exchange.

Finally, an end to the war might permit further diversification of Angola's economic relations away from the Eastern bloc. The treaty of friendship and cooperation signed with the USSR in 1976 has so far resulted in only small amounts of economic aid, mainly in fisheries and agriculture. As of 1982 (the latest year for which statistics are available), only 2 percent of Angola's exports went to the countries of the Council for Mutual Economic Assistance (CMEA), and only 7 percent of its imports came from there.

The socialist countries have significant toeholds in certain sectors, however, and these do not always work to Angola's benefit. The USSR's fishing agreement with Angola is a case in point. The fishing fleets reportedly scoop up everything in sight, including immature fish, threatening the future of the stocks. The Soviets reportedly agreed recently to sell more of the fish in Angolan markets. Meanwhile, some fishing contracts with the Soviets are not being renewed as they expire, and new deals are being negotiated with Spanish partners willing to market still higher proportions of the catch locally.

These problems may partly explain why Angola has irritated East Germany by accepting the so-called Berlin Clause in the EEC's Lomé Convention and perhaps why it has not joined the CMEA (although the latter omission may be due to decisions made in Eastern Europe rather than Luanda).

Angola is not entirely unhappy with its economic relationship with the socialist countries, however, and is particularly appreciative of their flexibility on debt payments. On balance, it is probably safe to assume that if the MPLA did not need to remain in the good graces of the socialist countries in order to ensure a regular supply of arms and other assistance vital to its defensive war against UNITA and South Africa, it might not continue to accept some of the disadvantageous terms of trade in its economic relations with these allies. For the time being, however, any major changes remain fantasies.

5

Cuba and Angola

Gillian Gunn

March 1987

Cuban relations with Angola have gone through several distinct phases. These phases have been marked by intermittent divergence between Soviet and Cuban interests in Angola, an emphasis by Havana on enhancing Cuban influence and national prestige, and generally, but not always, greater congruence between the interests of Havana and Luanda than between those of Luanda and Moscow. They also provide evidence that Cuban behavior over the years fits neither a leftist "Cuba as hero" nor a conservative "Cuba as villain" stereotype.

The Phases

Phase 1 ran from Fidel Castro's seizure of power in 1959 to the 1974 Lisbon coup that ended the long war between Portugal and nationalist guerrillas in Angola. During this period, Cuban relations with one of the three major Angolan nationalist groups, the MPLA, blossomed from a cautious friendship to a full-fledged alliance. Contrary to the conventional wisdom in the West, the increasing Cuban involvement with the MPLA at this early stage was not initiated on Soviet advice; indeed, relations between Havana and Moscow became uneasy between 1962 and 1968 because of disagreements over the handling of the 1962 missile crisis, the role of revolutionary guerrilla movements in the Third World, and Soviet rhetoric about peaceful coexistence with the United States. This Havana-Moscow tension strengthened Castro's desire to reach out to ideologically compatible revolutionary movements, such as the MPLA, to enhance his international influence and independence. A trusting friendship grew up between Castro and MPLA leader Agostinho Neto.

Although a 1968 slowdown of Soviet oil deliveries persuaded Castro to mend his fences with Moscow, Cuba continued to champion Neto's cause even when MPLA fissures caused the USSR in 1973 to shift support temporarily to Daniel Chipenda, leader of a dissident MPLA faction. The Chipenda episode highlighted the differences between Cuban and Soviet priorities in Angola during this era. For Castro, ideological and Third World solidarity, as well as personal loyalty to Neto, were paramount. For the USSR, the most important considerations were Neto's ability to gain power and indications as to whether he would be receptive to Soviet requests once in power. When both of these prospects became less certain, Moscow sought out alternative horses to back.

Phase 2 began with the Portuguese coup in April 1974 and ran to the consolidation, with Soviet and Cuban help, of MPLA power in post-independence Angola in early 1976. Again, contrary to the conventional view, Cuba was neither *the* hero nor *the* villain of this critical period. South Africa, Cuba, and the United States roughly simultaneously – and largely secretly – increased their involvement in relatively independent decisions during the period from April 1974 to October 1975. As the results of these decisions were seen in the field, each of the governments involved – knowing the political alliances of the various Angolan actors – speculated that the other external powers were preparing to intervene directly, and responded accordingly. Only after October 1975 did each element's plans become clear, and lead to informed decisions rather than actions based on hunches. In this period, Cuban and Soviet interests overlapped more completely than in the first phase. But once again Cuban involvement was not simply that of a compliant Soviet surrogate; indeed, it was Castro who urged Moscow to become more committed to the struggle in Angola. On the other hand, Cuba obviously could not have carried out its Angolan operation as speedily or efficiently as it did had the Soviet Union not provided arms and transportation facilities.

Why was Cuba so anxious to leap to Neto's aid during the 1975 civil war? Castro's personal relationship with Neto, the traditional Cuban desire, magnified under Castro, to play an international role transcending the island's small size, and the opportunity to test the Cuban military in the "real world" were all factors. Although Cuba received improved trade terms from the USSR after the intervention, and profited financially in the civilian (though not necessarily in the military) sphere in Angola from 1976 to the early 1980s, economic incentives were too problematical at the outset to have played a significant role in Castro's 1975 decision to intervene.

Phase 3 extended roughly from 1976 to 1981. In this period the Cuban military role in Angola shifted from that of an expeditionary force to an indefinite presence. Planned withdrawal of Cuban combat forces was halted as the security situation deteriorated. Tensions with Zaire generated in early 1977 by the abortive cross-border invasion into Shaba province by Katangan exiles living in Angola contributed to the policy reversal, as did a May 1977 coup attempt by an MPLA faction with apparent close Soviet ties. Cuba strongly backed Neto in the latter incident, while, at a crucial moment, the Soviet Union temporarily "sat on the fence."

As the Cubans prepared for the long haul in Angola, more precise guidelines defining their military role were worked out with the MPLA. The Cubans took on backup infrastructure and logistics activities, staying away from frontline combat with either UNITA or South Africa. Cuban civilian cooperation also increased dramatically, as evidenced by the arrival in Angola of large numbers of doctors, agricultural technicians, teachers, construction engineers, and other specialists. Some stresses arose between Angolan and Cuban personnel in both the military and civilian spheres over such issues as the modestly better living conditions enjoyed by the Cubans, but on the whole Cubans achieved much better individual rapport with Angolans than did their Soviet counterparts.

Why was Cuba willing to take on long-term commitments in Angola well beyond what was anticipated when the initial decision to send an expeditionary force was made? Cuba may have been offered material compensation for its military activities, permitting it to cover costs or even earn profits, though the record is still unclear on this issue. But even if compensation was not offered, other incentives beckoned. Increasing South African military activity within Angola brought Cuba the prestige-enhancing opportunity of presenting itself as a defender of blacks against white racists, an image Castro coveted. At the same time, the growing South African military presence in Angola increased the political cost of abandoning Neto, for Havana might then appear to other Third World leaders to be leaving the MPLA to the mercy of the apartheid regime. In addition, even if Cuba were not breaking even (or profiting) on its military activities in Angola, it certainly was gaining material compensation in the civilian sphere. Finally, long-term involvement in Angola promised to give Cuba important reverse leverage over the Soviet Union on both political and economic matters, a weapon Castro sorely needed. In Angola, the Cubans were performing a task the Soviets wanted done, but were unable or unwilling to do themselves. To a certain extent this enabled the Cuban "tail" to wag the Soviet "dog."

Phase 4 lasted roughly from 1981 to 1984. During this period, Cuban relations with the MPLA were placed under some strain by the latter's negotiations with the United

States and South Africa on terms for a phased Cuban withdrawal. The MPLA informed Havana only intermittently of the course of these discussions, seeming to put its own interest in peace before its ally's interest in maintaining prestige. Cuba did not oppose withdrawal in principal, but was extremely anxious that it be carried out in a manner that implied Cuban victory rather than defeat. The lack of consultation thus made Havana uneasy.

The 1981–1984 period also brought a reduction of Cuban earnings in Angola, for in 1983 Cuba waived payments for the services of its civilian personnel, an action presumably prompted by Luanda's cash-flow problems due to the increased costs of the war.

Phase 5 began in early 1985. It has been defined by the stalemate in U.S. (and South African) negotiations with the MPLA on the issue of Cuban troop withdrawal following South African attacks on Angolan territory and the U.S. decision to aid UNITA.

Although the 1985–1987 period has been marked by diplomatic paralysis, there has been some motion in MPLA and Cuban attitudes on withdrawal. For most of 1986, Cuban and MPLA positions were united in a hard-line stance. Whereas the two countries had previously tied withdrawal to the achievement of internationally recognized independence for Namibia and an end to South African support for UNITA, they now asserted that withdrawal would not take place until apartheid was overthrown. But by early 1987 the MPLA's public statements swung back to the former more flexible position, while Cuban rhetoric stuck with the new stance.

The difference might partly reflect a conscious "Mutt and Jeff" act, in which one party plays the "tough guy" and the other appears conciliatory. But it also seems to reflect a concrete shift of interests, with the MPLA focusing on its short-term interest in neutralizing South African aggression, while the increasing unrest within South Africa makes Castro more interested than previously in maintaining a foothold in the region for carrying out other (not necessarily military) operations, and as a venue for supportive contacts with the African National Congress. The tougher Cuban line may also reflect Castro's concern that Washington's 1986 decision to aid UNITA and ongoing South African military support of Jonas Savimbi's guerrilla army make Cuban withdrawal dangerous both for MPLA survival and for Havana's prestige.

Implications for U.S. Policy

The preceding description of Cuban policy in Angola has the following implications for U.S. dealings with the MPLA:

• If, as the historical record implies, Cuban policy on Angola is not simply set by Moscow, and can diverge somewhat from Soviet policy at times, then U.S. policymakers presumably cannot just negotiate with the USSR about Angola, but must take account of, and deal with, the Cuban point of view. While Washington-Moscow discussions are essential because no proposed solution for the Angolan situation will have much chance of success if the Soviets oppose it, any solution that does not respond to Cuba's special interests also risks failure.

• The history of Cuban involvement in Angola shows that Havana's most consistent interest is promotion of its international image and influence, and the fulfillment of a self-defined historical "mission." This suggests that U.S.-Soviet or U.S.-MPLA formulas for obtaining Cuban withdrawal must either provide a face-saving rationale for Cuba's departure, or include steps to neutralize the actions Cuba might take to hinder the negotiations.

• Events over the past few years suggest that the MPLA will, in general, put its own interests before those of the Cubans. This means that direct bilateral U.S.-MPLA contacts could be useful; though USSR and Cuban concerns must be addressed before a deal can be finalized, such bilateral discussions could structure the diplomatic environment in a manner that would limit Soviet-Cuban options.

  • The evidence shows that Cuba is currently benefiting less than previously from its economic involvement in Angola. Yet the willingness to remain seems undiminished. This suggests that the United States should not expect the deterioration of the MPLA's financial fortunes due to war and the collapse of the oil price to lead to a reduction of Cuban commitment to MPLA defense.

  • The evidence further suggests that among the main factors strengthening Cuba's willingness to stay in Angola have been the deterioration of South African internal stability and increased South African threats to the region, and that U.S. aid to UNITA has reinforced the decision. U.S. policymakers should, therefore, expect that the more southern Africa is inflamed, the more interest Cuba will take in the region. This in turn suggests that the United States should seek to promote regional stability (e.g., by aiding some of South Africa's vulnerable neighbors) and should be prepared for increased Cuban "meddling" in the event that its efforts fail.

What Cuba Has Learned

The Cuban record in Angola also has implications for future Cuban "adventurism" elsewhere in southern Africa. Although outsiders can only speculate, it seems plausible that Cuba may have drawn the following conclusions from its Angolan experience:

  • No matter how rich a country may be in natural resources, and therefore how advantageous long-term military and trade partnerships may appear, internal instability and unpredictable movements in international commodity prices can transform those partnerships from financial assets into financial liabilities. Such developments can be partly offset by the extra bargaining power unprofitable "support of socialist-oriented countries" operations give Cuba in economic negotiations with the USSR, even though the connections cannot be viewed as long-term assets themselves.

• Economic and military realities in Africa are very different from those in Latin America. The underdeveloped nature of African economies, the complexities of African ethnic relationships, and the vastness of the African terrain (and, in the case of southern Africa, the proximity of a relatively well-developed regional superpower whose actions are not constrained by the norms of international behavior) all mean that military and economic management techniques appropriate to Latin America have to be carefully adapted to African conditions, and even then may not work well.

• Cuba has learned that, once having become militarily involved in a conflict, getting out without damaging one's own international status can prove extremely difficult. After Cuban troops arrive in the host country, they can become hostages to events controlled by other parties, and what is envisaged as a short-term military commitment can turn into an open-ended involvement (if prestige is not to be sacrificed).

• Cuban casualties abroad do eventually cause social problems at home. While they can be justified for a short-term operation, they are hard either to camouflage or to justify over the longer term.

• Military actions in third countries can bring about unintended conflicts with the Soviet Union when factionalism breaks out in the supported group. Thus, while the potential benefit of a military operation is that it can give Havana increased influence on Moscow, it can also create conflicts between the two countries that have the opposite result.

• A southern African ally is not likely to put Cuban interests first. In certain circumstances, local national priorities may threaten that most precious of commodities, Cuban prestige.

• Cuban civilian personnel have generally been well received in Angola. While there are occasional cultural and racial conflicts with the local populace, the record on civilian cooperation has generally enhanced Cuba's image.

• Taking a stand against South Africa is extremely popular in much of the Third World, and goes a long way toward offsetting criticism of Cuba's position on controversial issues such as Afghanistan.

Looking Ahead

If Cuba has drawn the above conclusions from its Angolan experience (a contention certainly open to debate), then what are the prospects for Cuban intervention elsewhere in southern Africa?

It is likely that Cuba will now think more carefully before getting as deeply involved militarily in, say, Mozambique or South Africa as it has in Angola. The difficulties associated with military "adventurism" – specifically the problem of surrendering control over crucial prestige-relevant aspects of diplomacy to the host government, the social effects of casualties, the intractable nature of African guerrilla conflicts, and the danger of getting pulled in deeper than originally intended – all seem better appreciated in Havana today than they were in the pre-Angola era.

The Angolan experience has also demonstrated how "fighting apartheid" can enhance one's prestige in the Third World. If the internal South African situation heats up, if Pretoria evidences increasing willingness to retaliate against neighbors for perceived aid to ANC infiltrators, and if the spotlight of international media attention focuses ever more intensely on the apartheid system, the attraction of looking like a "knight in shining armor" will be hard to resist.

Obviously, the preferred scenario from Cuba's point of view would be to play a "heroic" role without getting directly involved militarily. Since Cuba is not in a position to extend much financial aid, it must look to alternatives.

Training allies in the use of Soviet arms, while staying well
back from the front lines of the conflicts with or within
South Africa, is one option. If this option is pursued, maintenance of a Cuban military presence in Angola takes on
new meaning, as it offers a convenient site for contacts
between Cuba and the ANC. Sending civilian "humanitarian" personnel, such as doctors and teachers, to additional
states in the southern region and providing scholarships to
students from those states are other relatively risk-free options. Facilitating the "armed struggle" in South Africa by
providing technicians to help neighboring states rebuild
their infrastructures represents still another way of enhancing prestige and influence while avoiding the risks associated with massive military involvement. Finally, Cuba's
experience in training indigenous civilian personnel to act
as local militias may be useful for those southern African
states which fear attack by "dissidents" receiving South
African training and support. Again, this can be done without sending an actual combat force to the host country.

Discussion of lessons Cuba may have drawn from its
Angolan experience, and the way those lessons may affect
future Cuban policy in southern Africa, is obviously highly
speculative. The above suggestions should not be interpreted as concrete predictions. They do show, however, that
both "Cuba as villainous Soviet puppet" and "Cuba as independent hero" stereotypes fail to explain a wide range of
elements in past and present Cuban policy. If this is the
case in Angola, it may well be the case for Cuba in other
parts of the world. Thus simplistic assumptions about Cuban motivations in other regions should be constantly
checked against the daily reality of Cuban actions on the
ground. If analyses of Cuban policies are not conducted in
an atmosphere freed from the constraints of both left- and
right-leaning hysteria, Western responses may end up
enhancing rather than reducing Cuban influence.

II

Mozambique

6

Post-Nkomati Mozambique

Gillian Gunn

January 1985

Nearly 10 months after signing the March 16, 1984 Nkomati Accord with South Africa, Mozambique resembles the paradoxical patient whose operation is a success but whose medical status remains critical. If the patient succumbs, the experiment will have little chance of being repeated, and the prospects for peaceful coexistence between South Africa and its neighbors will diminish sharply.

Both parties to the Nkomati Accord agree that the "operation" is a success in the sense that the other signatory is living up to the letter of the Accord. South African officials affirm publicly that Mozambique has indeed ceased to provide logistical facilities for the military arm of the African National Congress, as pledged in the Accord. The government of Mozambique, for its part, accepts as fact that the South African government has suspended direct support for the guerrilla forces of the Resistência Nacional Moçambicana (known as Renamo or the MNR), again as pledged in the Accord.

Even so, Mozambique is faltering. MNR operations have escalated. The country's transport network is repeatedly mined; the capital is subjected to intermittent power sabotage; aid agencies are pulling their technicians out of the countryside to avoid MNR kidnappings and killings.

The Two Views of Nkomati

Although Nkomati was viewed as an important gain by both signatories, the reasons were not the same in Pretoria and Maputo. For South Africa, the opening of the door and formal implementation of the respective promises were reason enough. Mozambique, on the other hand, signed the pact primarily to produce one specific result – liquidation of the MNR guerrilla war against the government. The principal Mozambican negotiator, Minister for Economic Affairs in the President's Office Jacinto Veloso, warned in an October 6, 1984 interview: "If the bandit action does not stop, Nkomati will be put in jeopardy."

The threats to declare Nkomati a failure were intended to force South Africa to take a more active role in combating the MNR – to focus on ends as well as means. They generated a new level of action on the part of South Africa in the second half of 1984 that culminated in an apparent breakthrough on October 3. On that date, delegations representing the government of Mozambique and the MNR were present in the same hall in Pretoria as South African Foreign Minister Roelof ("Pik") Botha read the following statement (the so-called "Pretoria Declaration"):

(1) Samora Moises Machel is acknowledged as the President of the People's Republic of Mozambique.

(2) Armed activity and conflict within Mozambique from whatever quarter or source must stop.

(3) The South African government is requested to consider playing a role in the implementation of this declaration.

(4) A commission will be established immediately to work toward an early implementation of this declaration. Botha added that South Africa agreed to take part in the commission.

There was some initial confusion as to just what the Declaration meant. But it has now become clear that it marked a shift in the South African government's public attitude toward Nkomati. Pretoria implicitly recognized Mozambique's priorities in associating itself with the statement that "armed activity . . . must stop." A month later, the South African government underscored the distancing from the MNR by blocking a Pretoria press conference scheduled by the movement's representatives; meanwhile, South African newspapers began to give more attention to allegations of MNR atrocities. MNR spokesmen responded to these developments by labeling Foreign Minister Botha an "unconditional ally of the [Mozambican government]."

Maputo's initial public statements on the Pretoria Declaration enlarged upon its actual language, implicitly characterizing it as a cease-fire agreement or an MNR surrender. As Radio Mozambique rejoiced: "The fact that the representatives of organized banditry recognized President Samora Machel means the recognition of the government and all institutions of the People's Republic of Mozambique. . . . The result of these negotiations is the acceptance by the armed bandits that their actions lead nowhere."

Despite this public posture, the Mozambican negotiators knew that the Pretoria Declaration was a compromise. Machel had sent Veloso to Pretoria with a draft declaration of a unilateral cease-fire. Instead he got an ambiguous document, signed by none of the three parties.

The fact that the document was no armistice quickly became apparent. Within hours after the Pretoria Declaration was announced, the MNR sabotaged a key Maputo power line, forcing the capital to limp along on emergency power supplies for three days. After consulting with their delegation in Pretoria, MNR spokesmen in Lisbon announced that the struggle would continue, and insisted that the Declaration recognized Machel as Mozambique's president only until new elections could be held.

South Africa's Dual Agenda?

The Pretoria Declaration was significant in that it was South Africa's first public commitment to play a role in obtaining peace in Mozambique; but this is not to say that

Pretoria's position on the MNR was unequivocal. The evidence is pretty clear that some elements in the South African ruling establishment agreed to Nkomati with a dual agenda in mind. This faction assumed and intended that the MNR would remain an active element after the accord, and that the pressure of the guerrilla war would eventually force Machel to agree to negotiate a power sharing agreement. Whether with or without Prime Minister (now President) Botha's approval, sufficient arms appear to have moved across the border just before Nkomati to keep the MNR operating for some time – some observers say through the end of 1985. And somebody somewhere had to be deliberately looking the other way when elements of South Africa's significant Portuguese population (about 700,000, according to Portugal's Prime Minister Mario Soares), many of them emigrants who had fled Mozambique just after independence, arranged their own cross-border supply operation for the MNR.

Mozambican officials see the foot-dragging and ambivalence of South African policy in the early stages of Nkomati as a manifestation of a split within the Botha government. According to their scenario, the South African military, and particularly military intelligence, was reluctant to abandon the MNR, while a "moderate" group, represented by the Department of Foreign Affairs and Prime Minister Botha, signed Nkomati in good faith. President Machel believes that his government's interests will best be served by strengthening the hand of the relatively friendly elements in the South African government while weakening the hard-liners. Some South African journalists and analysts suggest that this explanation may be overly simplistic. "Thump and talk are not mutually exclusive," a Johannesburg academician reminded me, and "the Pretoria Declaration may simply be the latest twist in an ongoing two-track policy."

In any case, Maputo has challenged South Africa to demonstrate its genuine commitment to the success of the Nkomati Accord both by blocking any further unofficial supply shipments to the MNR and by meeting Machel's requests for three forms of military support: (1) SADF troops to protect vital infrastructure against MNR attacks; (2) sharing of detailed intelligence concerning the location of MNR arms caches and specific radio frequencies used for communication; and (3) sophisticated arms to assist in the counterinsurgency effort.

Pretoria has replied that it cannot, for reasons of both principle and limited supply, provide any materiel covered by the arms embargo imposed on South Africa by the UN Security Council in 1977. Although a small number of South African military advisors are reportedly helping strengthen protection of the Cabora Bassa dam complex, no moves have been made to send substantial numbers of troops. Intelligence coordination is increasing, but not sufficiently as yet to give the Mozambican military a decisive edge against the MNR.

The Portuguese Factor

South African ambivalence is not the only reason Nkomati has not met all of President Machel's expectations. Another problem is that Nkomati did not take account of all the actors in the drama, in particular the MNR's Portuguese benefactors. Indeed, Mozambican officials believe that Portuguese support for the MNR escalated after Nkomati, breathing new life into the guerrilla organization.

Machel first hinted publicly at Portuguese involvement in June 1984 when he referred to a "conspiracy against Mozambique's independence and sovereignty" involving "personalities of governments which maintain diplomatic relations with our country" and "circles nostalgic for colonialism." Since then, the diplomatic gloves have come off and the charges are more explicit. On October 21, 1984, *Domingo* published an article specifically accusing Portuguese Deputy Prime Minister Mota Pinto, Minister of State Almeida Santos, and industrialist Manuel Bulhosa of complicity with the MNR. Santos had owned property in Mozambique before independence. Bulhosa is the former owner of Mozambican oil refineries that were nationalized by the Machel regime and his Lisbon publishing operation employs two leading MNR figures, Evo Fernandes and Jorge Correia.

The decision to accuse Portugal was not taken lightly; indeed, the *Domingo* article was held up while the Ministry of Information pondered the implications of going public. The balance was tipped by reports of Portuguese meddling in the trilateral "technical commission" set up under the terms of the Pretoria Declaration. High-ranking officials in the Mozambican Ministry of Foreign Affairs contend that Evo Fernandes had been on the verge of agreeing to a cease-fire during the first commission meeting when Pinto telephoned from Lisbon, instructing him not to sign anything and to return to Portugal for consultations. Whatever the reasons, the MNR's negotiating position did indeed harden midway in the first commission session, and soon afterward the guerrilla group pulled out of the talks altogether.

South Africa, by this point publicly committed to the technical commission talks, agreed that the Portuguese role had been unhelpful, and Foreign Minister Botha undertook to visit Lisbon to discuss the matter with Bulhosa, Santos, Pinto, and Prime Minister Soares. As Botha prepared to board his plane on October 12, Pinto cancelled the visit, saying the timing was inconvenient. Diplomatic sources suggest that the Portuguese did not want Soares to be included in the discussions, as this would associate him too closely with the MNR controversy.

The tension then heightened, as the dispute moved from government-sanctioned newspaper commentary to formal diplomatic protest. On November 2, Mozambican Foreign Minister Joaquim Chissano called in the Portuguese ambassador and conveyed "the serious concern of the People's Republic of Mozambique over the involvement of Portuguese citizens and personalities in preparing and leading acts of banditry from Portugal against Mozambique."

"The free and unimpeded development of such criminal acts from Portuguese territory," Chissano added, "contradicts the principles of normal relationships between states and endangers the good relations between the two governments."

One piece of evidence lending credibility to the charges of a greater Portuguese role in MNR strategy formulation after Nkomati was a shift in the MNR's demands. In the pre-Nkomati period, the emphasis was on free elections, free enterprise, and nondiscrimination against neighbors with "different political systems," an agenda that reflected the priorities of the movement's South African patrons. Now the MNR is making what Mozambican officials call "colonial" demands – including the return of confiscated Portuguese properties. In mid-November 1984, the MNR sent letters to large numbers of colonial-era residents living in Lisbon, urging them to return to Mozambique and promising that their former property would be returned when the MNR comes to power. Officials in Maputo also attach significance to the new MNR demand for the return of the *regulado* system (a network of compliant chiefs who carried out Portuguese instructions in the colonial era) in the rural areas. Cited in further support of the Mozambican allegations is the August 1984 arrest of four Portuguese "game hunters" in Tanzania. The four, who remain in Tanzanian custody, are accused of preparing bases, including airstrips, to facilitate continued supplies of arms to MNR units operating in the north of Mozambique.

The Portuguese government's motivations for permitting the MNR to continue operating from Lisbon, and, if Mozambique's allegations are valid, for allowing businessmen to coordinate and finance the MNR, are somewhat baffling. Since 1975, successive governments have sought to solidify relations with the five lusophone ex-colonies in Africa. Although recognizing that it lacks the financial resources to undertake major initiatives in these countries, Lisbon has envisaged a growing role for Portugal as a channel for Western assistance and investment. The path recently taken in Mozambique would seem to place at risk the larger goal of a special relationship with lusophone Africa.

Even in the short run, the risks are considerable. Portugal has lost substantial revenue as a result of MNR sabotage of the Cabora Bassa power project, in which there is a Portuguese financial interest. Portuguese technicians have been kidnapped and killed, and Portuguese directors of private companies in Mozambique are now receiving threats and demands for protection money.

Some observers cite the MNR's anti-Portuguese activities as evidence that the Mozambican government's accusations of official Portuguese support for the guerrillas are unfounded. Mozambican officials turn this argument on its head. The reason the Portuguese government looks on impassively as the MNR "bandits" strike indiscriminately at Portuguese interests, a Mozambican journalist close to the negotiations explained to me, is that Portugal considers present investors in Mozambique as "second-class citizens" and is willing to sacrifice them in a psychological war designed to secure final victory for the MNR and long-term Portuguese interests.

A more likely explanation is that the Portuguese government and business community are not united on the MNR issue. One faction, represented by businessmen currently active in Mozambique and possibly by Prime Minister Soares himself, wants to move forward to a more sophisticated economic relationship with Mozambique, in which Portugal would be a middleman in aid and investment deals. This faction has an interest in stability in Mozambique and in maintaining good relations with the Machel government. It wants what one might call a "neocolonial" relationship.

On the other side are the Portuguese businessmen and officials who lost their properties and roles in Mozambique. Rather than move forward to a new economic relationship, they want to move back to an old one. They want to "recolonize" rather than "neocolonize." They believe that the MNR is on the verge of military victory, and believe it is worth a considerable gamble to replace the South Africans as the bankroller of the movement's operations. One Mozambican analyst offered this explanation: "We are seeing a delayed reaction. Had a viable opposition organization existed at the time of independence, [these displaced Portuguese] would have moved immediately. . . . Now, 10 years later, the opportunity to win back property and influence has presented itself, and this section of the Portuguese community is exploiting it. Mario Soares might want to control this faction, but he needs their support to maintain his majority in parliament, and so his hands are tied."

Other Friends of the MNR

Another factor undermining the Nkomati Accord is the support the MNR has enjoyed from Malawi and West Germany. Although not as crucial as the aid it received from South Africa, and apparently now receives from Portugal, this assistance is not insignificant.

The Malawi connection goes back many years. Orlando Cristina, secretary-general of the MNR until his death under mysterious circumstances in South Africa in April 1983, established close relations with Malawi's President H. Kamuzu Banda when he trained that country's "Young Pioneers" organization. Malawi subsequently permitted the MNR to infiltrate across its border into Mozambique. Like South Africa, Malawi is host to a large number of Portuguese who lost property in Mozambique, and these individuals provided some financing.

Malawi's enthusiasm for the MNR began to falter in 1983, however, as guerrilla activity blocked Malawian exports exiting by rail and road through Mozambique. The rail line between Blantyre and Beira, which formerly carried up to 60 percent of Malawi's exports and imports, has been closed since early 1983, forcing Malawi to reroute traffic via South Africa at up to four times the cost.

In October 1984, Machel decided to capitalize on Banda's unease over the MNR, and made his first official visit to Malawi. Mozambique did not get the specific security agreement it wanted, but the two neighbors did formulate a general cooperation agreement stating that their governments will "not allow their respective territories to be used as bases, or give support to any organization or group of people which intends or prepares itself to launch violent acts, terrorism, or aggression against the other." Despite this agreement, the Mozambican authorities apparently still believe that Malawian residents are supplying the MNR, not necessarily with the approval or knowledge of the government.

The West German connection appears to consist more of moral support than of direct aid. In 1983, Evo Fernandes was invited to an academic conference at Kiel University. The visit was set up by a German friend of Fernandes resident in South Africa, and permitted the MNR leadership to make contact with a number of politicians and businessmen. Since then, the MNR has received encouragement from these personalities, and may be receiving funds.

The MNR also has sympathizers in the United States. MNR members say that they have declined offers of funds and mercenary services from several U.S. "war magazines." The Washington-based Heritage Foundation and other conservative organizations have arranged meetings between MNR spokesmen and members of Congress. There is no evidence, however, that the MNR is receiving funding from any of these sources.

The FRELIMO Factor

Another major reason why Nkomati has not yet brought the peace envisaged is that the governing party of Mozambique, the Frente de Libertação de Moçambique (FRELIMO), made the mistake of placing all of the blame for the success of the MNR insurgency on the actions of outsiders. Like the Portuguese colonialists before it,

FRELIMO failed to recognize, until recently, that its own shortcomings inadvertently created fertile recruiting grounds for its enemies.

In what ways have FRELIMO actions (and failures to act) served the MNR's purposes? First, and perhaps most important, a combination of policy blunders and the worst drought in 50 years has resulted in widespread hunger in the countryside. After independence in 1975, FRELIMO undertook to manage every level of the food distribution system from the center. Thus, the hastily departed Portuguese petty traders were replaced by a network of People's Shops operating under a central administration. Too few shops were established and they were inefficient and poorly stocked in basic consumer goods. When peasants realized they could buy little with the currency they received for their crops, they not surprisingly began to revert to subsistence farming.

The policy of encouraging large state farms also helped to alienate the peasantry from the party. Although FRELIMO did not impose collectivization by force, the state farms' priority access to resources was a source of resentment in rural areas.

These misjudgments were partly a result of the increasingly urban orientation of the FRELIMO leadership. During the guerrilla war against the Portuguese, the FRELIMO leaders lived in the midst of the peasants, mainly in Cabo Delgado and Niassa provinces. Their very survival depended upon the goodwill of this rural constituency. Any peasant dissatisfaction was rapidly communicated, and rectifying the problem was given high priority by the party. When the FRELIMO leaders moved to Maputo after independence to take over operation of the central administration, they gradually fell out of touch with their rural constituents. It would be unfair to criticize FRELIMO too harshly for this breakdown; black education in the colonial period was so limited that only a small number of FRELIMO cadres had the training for administering a government and few could be spared for rural administration.

Western diplomats long resident in Mozambique also

point out that FRELIMO support in those rural areas not directly controlled by the party during the "liberation struggle" never ran as deep as in Cabo Delgado and Niassa. Many areas of the country, while grateful for the independence FRELIMO won, did not closely identify with party goals.

A range of policy excesses have also contributed to growing rural, as well as urban, apathy toward FRELIMO. Party leaders admit that individuals were sometimes arrested on suspicion of counterrevolutionary activity and then, perhaps more out of disorganization than malice, were left to sit in jail for several years without being tried. Some well-intentioned political campaigns that backfired included "Operation Production," a 1984 undertaking to move unemployed from the cities, where they were contributing to the rising crime rate, to rural areas where it was hoped that they would be able to farm. The scheme was executed in a heavy-handed manner; selection of candidates was haphazard, and many men were separated from their families.

The military also must share some of the blame for the present state of affairs. During the war against the Portuguese, the FRELIMO guerrilla army was highly politicized. Although some guerrilla leaders remained in the army after independence, many, as noted above, moved to positions in the central government. The lower ranks have increasingly been comprised of younger, poorly educated recruits whose level of national consciousness is not comparable with that of the rank and file of the war years. Violent incidents with civilians, of a kind that would never have occurred when the force was highly politicized at all levels, have diminished the military's image (and thus FRELIMO's) in the countryside.

While FRELIMO is now taking energetic steps to right previous errors of omission and commission (see the section below on economic reform initiatives), a number of their consequences linger. The matter of peasant apathy toward the government is especially worrisome. Many in the rural areas of the country still nominally support FRELIMO,

but their loyalty to the party is overshadowed by their desire to live unmolested, and their awareness that the MNR
is not gentle with those who stand in its way. (Even sympathetic South African sources admit that the guerrillas have
been alarmingly brutal. Mutilation of ears, lips, and breasts
is common, particularly when units operate outside their
home territories.) An advisor to Machel has summed up the
situation in the following words: "[The peasants] feel the
road to the city doesn't bring anything. Therefore they are
not willing to risk their lives to prevent the MNR from
mining it."

A second fact of life is that the food shortage, caused in
part by inappropriate agricultural policies, has impelled
some young men to join the MNR—not out of political con-
viction, but because it is the only available alternative to a
hopeless existence in their villages. And finally, FRELIMO's
uneven performance has inevitably created a small but significant breakaway group from its own ranks with specific
grudges against the party leadership.

Can the MNR Be Isolated?

President Machel's most immediate objective is to get
South Africa more actively committed to Nkomati. There
are a number of conflicting pressures influencing Pretoria's
decision making on this issue. First, President Botha must
consider his country's economic interests. South Africa
needs new markets in black Africa for its goods if the current economic slump is to be ended, and a market as con-
veniently located as Mozambique is especially worth cultivating. It is for this reason that Maputo has been flooded,
since the signing of the Nkomati Accord, with South African businessmen bringing suggestions for joint projects.
South Africans are helping rehabilitate port and railroad
facilities, in part because improved transport would once
again permit goods from the Transvaal to exit through Ma-

puto – a much shorter route than the Richards Bay alternative. Farmers from South Africa's lowveld area are investigating agricultural investment opportunities in Mozambique, and various South African entrepreneurs are looking into the possibility of developing tourism on Mozambique's Inhaca Island. South Africa had always maintained some economic relations with Mozambique, even when political tensions were at their highest, but Nkomati set in motion a new level of activity.

South African businessmen, like other potential investors, realize that major investments or extensive operations in Mozambique will not be feasible until the security situation is brought under control. Therefore they are anxious that Nkomati succeed. Machel is dexterously playing off the business interests of these entrepreneurs against any ambivalence in Pretoria. He has ensured that Botha now faces a business pressure group that would complain vigorously if promising new opportunities were sabotaged due to official foot-dragging.

Another factor influencing thought in Pretoria is the example that a successful Nkomati follow-through would set for relations with the rest of Africa. If Nkomati brings peace to Mozambique, the Botha government will be in a much stronger position to persuade other African states that it is to their benefit to enter into similar accords. Pretoria knows that Angola's MPLA government, in particular, is watching carefully to see if South Africa truly does put a leash on the MNR. One of the thornier issues in the ongoing negotiations between Luanda and Pretoria is South Africa's long record of support for the guerrilla forces of Jonas Savimbi's UNITA.

There is a reverse side to the Angola analogy that the Botha government also must take into account – the effect leashing the MNR would have upon UNITA's morale. Though Pretoria may be prepared to cut support to UNITA (if by so doing it could obtain withdrawal of Cuban troops from Angola and an acceptable settlement in Namibia), it does not want to lose (or even damage) the UNITA lever until key South African goals are achieved.

And even if South Africa should decide to throw in its full lot with Machel, other considerations might rule out sending in military units to help suppress the MNR. The United States opposes in principle moves that involve foreign troops in the countries of southern Africa, and is also concerned that Scandinavian countries might react by reducing aid to Mozambique. This is no small matter, since more than 90 percent of the budget of Mozambique's Ministry of Agriculture is provided by Scandinavian aid. According to diplomatic sources, Sweden is already unhappy with Mozambique's recent decision to spend some of its aid money on South African goods in violation of the fine print in the Swedish aid agreement. Sweden is considering focusing on aid projects in the north of Mozambique, because it believes that projects in the south are more likely to be pulled into the South African economic system.

Given these conflicting pressures on the Botha government, the most Machel can realistically expect in the medium run may be some extra intelligence help and more careful monitoring of the border.

Mozambique would also like to isolate the MNR from its Portuguese backers. Machel has reportedly threatened to move his embassy in Lisbon to Madrid, and Mozambique could eventually adopt the Angolan tactic of excluding Portuguese companies from business contracts. But whatever decisions are taken at the official level, there are limits to the power of the Portuguese government to reduce significantly support by private citizens for the MNR. If Bulhosa is indeed financing the MNR, he could continue to do so via his investments in Brazil.

It will also be hard to seal off Malawian support entirely. Even if Banda signs a full-fledged security agreement and makes a concerted effort to control infiltration, some materiel will probably leak through. A large section of Malawi's border with Mozambique runs through the middle of

Lake Malawi, so fishing boats leaving from one shore can easily change course and head for the neighboring country.

Economic Reform

At FRELIMO's Fourth Congress, held in April 1983, a long period of rethinking within the party culminated in a massive shift in economic policy. FRELIMO committed itself to increasing the role of the private sector, shifted emphasis from large-scale to small- and medium-scale projects, decentralized economic management, and, most important, moved the agricultural focus from state farms to smaller-scale production units. The "family" sector was given special priority, with small cooperatives and private farmers also gaining greater access to funds. The government now places higher priority on supplying consumer goods to the rural areas, so that farmers will have an incentive to produce. Mozambique recently persuaded the USSR and Sweden to provide large shipments of consumer goods to stock rural shops.

Since the Fourth Congress, FRELIMO has implemented other realpolitik changes. In September 1984, in a sharp turn from previous policy, Mozambique became a member of the International Monetary Fund (which the Mozambican press in the immediate postindependence period had portrayed in cartoons as a well-fed businessman feeding poison to an African baby through a bottle). Mozambique is currently entitled to an IMF quota of approximately $60 million. It is immediately entitled to draw its "reserve tranche," which returns the foreign exchange it has contributed to the Fund in the process of joining. According to sources in the Bank of Mozambique, both the first and second tranches, each equal to about 25 percent of the total quota, will shortly be drawn. The first tranche has virtually no conditions attached, while the second has modest conditionality.

Membership in the IMF also entitles Mozambique to

membership in the World Bank and the International Finance Corporation. A $100 million World Bank loan was negotiated earlier in 1984 and a team has been sent in to evaluate the economy. A Bank study reportedly will recommend that almost all the Bank's grants be directed to the private sector.

The decision to join the IMF is of more than passing interest in light of previous associations. Mozambique has had observer status in the Soviet-dominated Council for Mutual Economic Assistance (CMEA), but was never offered full membership despite repeated hints of its desire to join. Perhaps a certain amount of pique underlay a remark by one official that Mozambique found that it could be admitted to the IMF as "an equal" with other members, whereas in the CMEA it was a "second-class citizen."

Mozambique has exhibited increasing flexibility in its negotiations with the so-called Paris Club. On October 29, 1984, the rescheduling of about $300 million in debts owed to Western governments was announced. The Paris Club agreed to postpone payments due in 1983, 1984, and the first half of 1985 to the 1990–1996 period. The basis for the agreement is an "action program" outlining Mozambique's targets for exports, imports, policies on prices and wages, and the exchange rate. Although details have not been made public, Maputo reportedly agreed to fairly stringent terms, with a 50 percent currency devaluation due in March 1985. Mozambique will also link its currency more closely to the South African rand; this reflects the expectation that economic ties with South Africa will grow. The rescheduling exercise is still not complete, since Mozambique has over $1 billion in remaining debt to renegotiate. But the reforms outlined in the "action program" are probably sufficient to meet the IMF's conditionality demands for access to Mozambique's second tranche.

Mozambique has also taken a more liberal attitude toward foreign investment. On July 28, 1984, it signed an agreement with the U.S. government's Overseas Private Investment Corporation (OPIC), a move neighboring Zimbabwe has thus far resisted. The agreement provides for bilateral investment guarantees to U.S. investors. In 1985 Mozambique will become a member of the Lomé Convention, the vehicle through which European Economic Community aid is channeled to the Third World.

A new investment code published on September 6, 1984 guarantees compensation for nationalization, permits nationalization only in "exceptional circumstances," and guarantees transfer of profits and repatriation of capital. This followed by only a few weeks a new law on the management of foreign exchange that allows enterprises (state, private, and foreign) to retain a portion of foreign exchange earned by exports. The funds can be spent on import of essential materials and on bonuses for workers. The move has been welcomed by the private sector, and represents a significant step away from centralized state control.

Similar pragmatism was evident in 1983, when Mozambique introduced a new code to govern oil exploration. Oil companies cite it as one of the most generous in the Third World, and have responded positively. Esso and Shell started exploration in May 1983 in the Rovuma Basin in the northeastern province of Cabo Delgado. In October 1984, an agreement was signed with AMOCO (Standard Oil of Indiana) covering four blocks in the Zambezi delta area between Quelimane and Beira. In November, British Petroleum signed an exploration contract covering 10,000 square kilometers from just south of Maputo to Xaixai in Gaza Province. Oil company sources in Mozambique report that initial surveys are more promising than originally anticipated and that there are also large proven reserves of natural gas.

Mozambique recognizes that it cannot change its economy from a service-based to a semi-industrialized one overnight. Whereas past rhetoric emphasized the desire to reduce economic ties with South Africa, current rhetoric concedes the economic logic of these links. In addition to the tourism and agricultural investment potential discussed earlier, Mozambique has requested that South Africa accept more mine labor. The reduction of the number of Mozambicans in South Africa's mines from 120,000 before independence to around 45,000 by 1984 cost Mozambique some $568 million. South Africa has now agreed to allow 8,000 more Mozambican miners to take jobs in the Republic in 1985. Mozambique is also actively encouraging South Africa to redirect freight through the port of Maputo. South African tonnage sent through Maputo dropped from 6.8 million in 1973 to an estimated 1 million in 1983. Finally, Mozambique is encouraging South Africa to buy more power from the Cabora Bassa Dam complex. Pretoria has agreed to pay a higher tariff, with a premium if a reliable supply is maintained.

Rejuvenation of the economy could also be helped by more Western aid. After the signing of the Nkomati Accord, a ban on U.S. bilateral nonemergency aid to Mozambique imposed by Congress in the late 1970s was lifted by presidential waiver. In late September 1984, one day before the U.S. fiscal year ended, an $8 million bilateral program was approved by Congress. A Commodity Import Program designed to support the private agricultural sector accounts for $6 million of the funds. This will provide foreign exchange for basic inputs such as fertilizer, seeds, hoes, tractors, and (primarily) spare parts. The remaining $2 million will be spent on technical assistance, and part will go through Portugal as "trilateral" aid. Mozambique was the world's largest recipient of U.S. food assistance in FY 1983 and 1984 – receiving approximately $30 million each year. Private charitable programs added another $10 million to the U.S. total in 1984.

Future U.S. aid almost certainly will depend partly upon Mozambique's willingness to maintain what Western diplomats call its "new genuinely nonaligned stance." On this score, Washington has been encouraged by the relatively moderate tone of Foreign Minister Chissano's October 1984 UN speech. But the United States may have problems with the Mozambican definition of nonalignment. The Machel government does not view nonalignment as a position equidistant from the two superpowers, in the Yugoslavian tradition. It believes that the socialist countries are indeed the natural allies of the Third World, as in the Cuban definition of nonalignment. Unlike Cuba, however, Mozambique insists that the socialist orientation does not imply an obligation to cooperate closely with the East's "military bloc."

Even if all the new economic reforms, investment incentives, and aid appeals go well, it will be several years before Mozambique's economic emergency ends. The government predicts that imports will be more than three times larger than exports in 1985, and will remain more than double the amount of exports in 1986. Before the recent debt rescheduling, debt service payments were due to rise by 80 percent by 1987, and would begin to fall only in 1991. The debt problem is postponed slightly with the new rescheduling, but post-1990 payments will be very heavy.

In addition, the country's exports are subject to price fluctuations in the international market. The main products are shrimp, cotton, sugar, timber, coal, cement, citrus, and small amounts of petroleum by-products. The prices for these goods fell by 31 percent between 1980 and 1982.

A FRELIMO-MNR Accommodation?

The preceding analysis implies that neither attempts to cut off the MNR's external support nor economic reform can assure the rebels' defeat, at least in the short run. One of the remaining alternatives is to engage in political negotiations with "the bandits." There are several problems inherent in this strategy.

First, FRELIMO unity was somewhat strained by the Nkomati signing, and could be pushed to the breaking point by a decision to negotiate with the MNR. In the years before Nkomati, FRELIMO did not implement decisions until full consensus was obtained. In a manner reminiscent of conflict resolution in traditional African societies, the party would engage in weeks of debate until all dissidents were convinced, or at least stopped pushing their arguments. In contrast, the early negotiations on Nkomati were discussed by a small group of FRELIMO leaders, and many high-ranking individuals were only informed in the closing stages. Some were unconvinced, and Armando Guebuza, then minister of the interior, was particularly indiscreet in voicing his opposition even after the signing. In June he was divested of the interior portfolio and, after a three-month period in limbo, shifted to a lesser post as minister of state in the President's Office. The official explanation was that he had implemented Operation Production in a particularly brutal manner, but Maputo-based diplomats are convinced the disagreement over Nkomati was the trigger. Guebuza is charismatic, has good relations with the army, and is one of the few FRELIMO figures who could conceivably rival Machel for the allegiance of the "masses."

A second block to negotiating with the MNR is uncertainty concerning the movement's composition. The MNR is apparently breaking into two distinct groups, one in the south and one in the north, with the center of Mozambique relatively quiet. The South Africans were most closely associated with the southern group, and could help Mozambique force this part of the MNR to live up to any agreement. The northern faction is far more independent, however, and appears to be well supplied (presumably from Portugal and Malawi). FRELIMO has no assurance that the northerners would live up to promises made by the southerners or vice versa.

There is also speculation concerning a split between the political and military leadership. Evo Fernandes and Jorge Correia, both whites with Portuguese passports, are viewed as political spokesmen, while Afonso Dhlakama, a black Mozambican sometimes called "Jacama" and carrying the title "Commander in Chief," is viewed as "military." FRELIMO noted that Dhlakama was present for the negotiations preceding the Pretoria Declaration, but did not appear in the hall when the Declaration was read, and has not been present in any of the negotiations since. FRELIMO questions whether he would respect any accord signed with Fernandes and/or Correia. Would he be in a position to continue fighting independently?

A third problem concerns the vagueness and contradictory nature of MNR demands. One week the organization announces that it will not talk to FRELIMO until it is recognized as an equal partner and until FRELIMO agrees to discuss substantive political issues. The next week it says President Machel need only admit that he is indeed talking to the MNR (an admission FRELIMO has been reluctant to make). The demands also seem to depend on the geographic location of the MNR representative doing the talking. Portuguese-based spokesmen emphasize the return of nationalized properties, while those in the United States focus on a call for new elections. FRELIMO does not know if these changes and contradictions represent the views of different factions within the MNR, or shifting positions of a united leadership. Other outside observers are little better informed.

Despite these difficulties, FRELIMO has considered doing a deal with the black rank and file of the MNR and excluding only the white leadership. (It has already offered an amnesty to guerrillas who surrender, which a small number have taken up.) Another possibility would be to offer low-level administrative posts to middle-ranking MNR leaders, though this would be bitterly opposed by some in FRELIMO. A third alternative involves persuading South Africa to take on large numbers of MNR guerrillas as mining laborers, to be repatriated one year later. Under this alternative, Mozambique would also expect South Africa, Portugal, and other Western countries to fund resettlement of the white MNR leadership in third countries.

The problem with all these deals is that they do not respond to the MNR's main concern: power sharing. Machel cannot go much further in meeting the MNR's demands without threatening party unity. And with its current military successes, the MNR sees no need to be flexible.

7

What Does the Case of Mozambique Tell Us About Soviet Ambivalence Toward Africa?

Winrich Kühne

August 1985

Developments in southern Africa since early 1984 have raised a range of new questions about Soviet policy and Soviet relevance in this region of the continent. In the military sphere, Soviet assistance has enabled neither Mozambique nor Angola to quell or even substantially diminish domestic guerrilla challenges that have blocked economic growth. There have also been growing doubts about the effectiveness in practical terms of orthodox state-centered Marxist-Leninist models of development—especially in agriculture, the most important socioeconomic sector of African states.

Meanwhile, an increasing number of Soviet analysts and strategists are questioning how much emphasis can or should be placed on ideology in cultivating relationships with Africa. Significantly, they categorize even the most pro-Soviet African governments as "of socialist orientation" rather than genuinely "socialist." Even among East German academicians, who in the past have often been more ideologically orthodox in their writing on developing countries than their Soviet counterparts, a fierce debate is going on about the circumstances under which there is still hope for a successful implementation of true socialism.

Frustrations are not confined to the area of ideology.

Eastern bloc economists have been forced into a far-reaching change of mind about the present global economy, and the risks of pursuing an uncompromising antagonistic policy against the world economic order and its main protagonists, the Western industrialized countries. In the southern African microcosm there are some intriguing signals that the East-West conflict, whose unbridled antagonism in the military sphere has already become outdated because of the mutual capacity for assured nuclear destruction, could move toward a modus vivendi in the Third World because of economic forces.

One indication of a Soviet policy shift – or, at least, ambivalence – was Moscow's subdued response to the signing on March 16, 1984 of a "nonaggression and good neighborliness" accord by the leaders of Mozambique and South Africa. Under the terms of the Nkomati Accord, Mozambique undertook to curb drastically the activities of the African National Congress (ANC), while South Africa promised to end assistance to the dissident MNR movement.

Although there is no doubt that Nkomati was seen by the Soviets as a negative development, Moscow did not retaliate by cutting aid to the government of President Samora Machel or recalling advisors. On December 26, 1983, with Nkomati already an inevitable event, the Soviet ambassador in Maputo, Yuri Sepelev, publicly stated that it was essential to understand that Mozambique was a sovereign state and "nobody's puppet." The Soviet Union, he said, understood Mozambique's desire to improve its relations "in all directions." To prove that this was not just a rhetorical position, Sepelev announced that more shiploads of rice and oil would arrive and also drew attention to a recently signed $300 million trade agreement. Only a few days after Nkomati was signed, Sepelev announced further Soviet loans, and the USSR was the first creditor to agree to reschedule Mozambique's debt after a worldwide appeal by President Machel.

Meanwhile, the Soviet Union has made no real effort to impede another key development in Mozambique – a so-called "opening to the West" that has involved not only economics but also politics, ideology, and even military affairs.

Strictly speaking, the use of the term "opening to the West" in connection with recent developments in Mozambique is somewhat misleading, because Western influence has never been completely excluded from the country. Since independence in 1975, the policy of the ruling party, FRELIMO, toward nonsocialist countries has been marked by pragmatism. South Africa and the Western industrialized countries have remained major trading partners; in 1979 they purchased about 80 percent of Mozambique's exports. It is true that the Eastern bloc countries increased their share of Mozambique's trade after independence, but one should keep in mind that they started more or less from zero. In 1980, East Germany was Mozambique's most important Eastern European trading partner, providing 9.5 percent of imports and receiving 8.1 percent of exports.

Although Mozambique's economic relations with the West were based on "pragmatism" and "realism" from the outset, FRELIMO's rhetoric was pro-Soviet and anticapitalist. In 1977, FRELIMO's Third Congress codified the decision to commit the country to a rather orthodox kind of Marxism-Leninism. FRELIMO announced its own transformation from a national liberation movement into a Marxist-Leninist vanguard party (even though a proletarian working class, the supposedly indispensable political basis of any such party, hardly existed in Mozambique). While FRELIMO expressly repudiated the idea of a "third way" between Western capitalism and Eastern bloc communism, this did not prevent President Machel from remaining on good political terms with Tanzania's President Julius Nyerere, an old friend and Machel's main protector during the liberation struggle.

The governing party's formal adherence to an orthodox Marxist-Leninist line did not imply an acceptance by Mozambique of Soviet ideological or military hegemony. Indeed, the leadership has repeatedly asserted the country's "national" independence in no uncertain terms. In particular, Machel has consistently refused to grant Soviet warships basing rights in the country's harbors. Soviet military vessels are granted only restricted access to certain facilities on an occasional basis. To make the message very clear to everybody, the principle of not allowing any foreign military bases ("with no exception") is enshrined in the 1978 constitution.

The South African Connection

Operating on the often-cited principle that nations can choose their friends but not their neighbors, Machel maintained a range of economic links with South Africa established while Mozambique was under Portuguese rule. After independence in 1975, South Africa quietly continued to help the FRELIMO government operate the port in Maputo and the country's railway. A formal cooperation agreement between the two countries (negotiated in secret and not mentioned in Mozambique's media) was signed on February 26, 1979.

Relations deteriorated sharply after 1980, however, as South Africa began a series of raids and other military actions into neighboring states in retaliation for ANC operations within the Republic believed to have been launched from external bases in the region. By striking directly against what it claimed were ANC buildings in Matola (on the outskirts of Maputo) in January 1981, and by imposing a 10-day rail embargo against Mozambique in March 1981 for "technical reasons," Pretoria left no doubt that it was dead serious about ending Mozambique's support for anti-apartheid liberation fighters. Meanwhile, MNR sabotage had resulted (according to a February 3, 1984 broadcast by Maputo radio explaining the reasons for entering into the Nkomati Accord) in the destruction of much of the nation's fledgling infrastructure, including key bridges, railway sections, pipelines, electric power stations, 586 schools, and 900 rural shops.

Speaking at the tenth meeting of the FRELIMO Central Committee in 1982, Machel provided the first indication that the answer to the MNR problem might have to involve compromise with Pretoria. Asserting that "South Africa recruits and trains, finances and equips, arms and organizes . . . the mercenaries and armed bands that operate in Mozambique," he called for "developing a broad movement of people's militias, training and arming the millions of Mozambican workers" to assist the army in fighting the MNR. A few sentences later, however, Machel hinted that such a strategy might not be adequate to save Mozambique and that a retreat on the antiapartheid front might be required to secure survival. He called for more "sophisticated weapons" to fight apartheid, but the kind of weapons he then proceeded to name – UNESCO conferences and protest concerts – camouflaged what he must clearly have had in mind: a scaling down of ANC activities. In fact, "sophistication" was another word for a retreat forced upon Machel by the geographical, historical, security, and economic circumstances his government faced. At about the same time, Mozambique signaled to the State Department in Washington that it would welcome U.S. assistance in reaching a fundamental accommodation with South Africa on questions of mutual security. These moves were the beginning of the process of negotiation that led in due course to the Nkomati Accord, which in effect recognized the political struggle in South Africa as a domestic issue.

The East's Contribution to Nkomati

It would be a mistake to conclude that Pretoria's destabilization policy was the pivotal factor in bringing about FRELIMO's rapprochement with the West. If one takes into account Mozambique's relations with the East, the picture becomes much more complicated. The change of mind toward the West was brought about not only by South Africa's stepped-up destabilization efforts in the early 1980s, but also by the rejection of Mozambique's endeavor during the same period to move from observer status to full membership in the Soviet-dominated Council for Mutual Economic Assistance (CMEA).

Why did Moscow rebuff Maputo on this issue? One reason was the financial burden already presented to the CMEA by Vietnam, Laos, and Cuba. Another was the difficulty of integrating Mozambique's economy with those of the other members. In any event, the consequences for Mozambique of its exclusion from full membership were clear: the comprehensive socialist, Marxist-Leninist orientation of FRELIMO's current program had presupposed integration into the Eastern bloc economic system and could not be sustained if such integration were not to materialize. Thus, Machel had to seek new partners and a new outlook.

Ideological Shifts, 1982–1984

By 1982, a process of rapid change was clearly evident in Mozambique's relations with the international community. In April of that year, Maputo signed a treaty of military cooperation with its former colonial oppressor, Portugal; there were also rumors of military cooperation with France and Britain. In August 1982, the Mozambican government for the first time recognized West Germany's claim to West Berlin in a food aid agreement with West Germany. This was an important symbolic step away from a longtime stance of "socialist solidarity" with East Germany (reportedly the only CMEA country to support Maputo's application for full membership). The previous Mozambican rejection of the "Berlin clause" had cut the country off from the flow of bilateral West German and multilateral EEC development aid. Shortly thereafter, Maputo announced its willingness to take part in the Lomé III negotiations, thereby beginning its formal reintegration into the Western economic system.

In August 1982, Mozambique concluded its first trade agreement with China (with which FRELIMO had had amicable relations during the independence struggle), thereby revitalizing its connection with another important country opposed to the spread of Soviet influence in southern Africa. Meanwhile, U.S. food aid increased from 43,000 tons in 1982 to a projected 350,000 tons for the 1984 fiscal year, and in 1984 Mozambique received more U.S. emergency food aid than any other country. In 1984 Mozambique also joined the Lomé Convention, the IMF, and the World Bank (which approved a loan of $45 million in June, 1985).

In April 1983, FRELIMO's Fourth Congress reached a series of important decisions concerning the country's future political and economic orientation. Moving toward the example set by Afro-socialist one-party systems, it de-emphasized the importance of "proletarian class struggle" as the ideological justification for FRELIMO's leadership, while strengthening the dominant role of the party and the centralized leadership. The most important developments were the modification, or more precisely the correction, of orthodox Marxist-Leninist elements of Mozambique's economic policy. Economic planning and implementation were decentralized, and agricultural development was redirected away from state farms with more support planned for small-scale family farming. (Soviet-style state farms had in most cases proved to be costly failures in terms of productivity.)

The Fourth Congress initiatives were followed by a new investment code that came into force on September 6, 1984. This new code not only facilitates joint ventures involving foreign and Mozambican state and private capital but allows for the establishment of wholly foreign-owned companies, which are offered safeguards with respect to nationalization and a guaranteed right to transfer their profits out of the country in hard currency.

The Failure of Soviet Military Aid

The steady deterioration of Mozambique's security during the pre-Nkomati period offered a classic situation of conflict and instability of the kind that (at least according to a widespread school of thought in the West) Moscow would not hesitate to use to its advantage. Why, then, was the Kremlin either unwilling or unable to exploit matters by increasing FRELIMO's dependence on Eastern bloc military assistance?

Article Four of the Treaty of Friendship and Cooperation concluded by the Soviet Union and Mozambique in March 1977 states: "In the interests of reinforcing the defense potentials of the High Contracting Parties, they will continue developing cooperation in the military sphere on the basis of appropriate agreements." Similar clauses about military cooperation appear in Mozambique's treaties with other Eastern bloc countries, including those with Cuba (October 1977) and East Germany (February 1979).

But, as was the case with economic cooperation, Machel and others in FRELIMO's leadership gradually became disenchanted about the utility of the close military alliance with the Eastern bloc countries. In February 1981, about two weeks after the attack by South African commandos on alleged ANC buildings in Matola, one cruiser and three smaller units of the Soviet Indian Ocean fleet visited Maputo and Beira. Valentin Vdovin, the Soviet ambassador in Maputo, told the press that these ships were meant to demonstrate Soviet solidarity with Mozambique against further attacks by South Africa. His public remarks created the impression that Moscow had decided to take a much tougher stand concerning South Africa's aggressiveness, but little happened in the following months apart from further regular visits by Soviet ships.

In May and June 1982, the increasingly precarious security situation within Mozambique triggered a flurry of visits to the Soviet Union and talks on security questions. In rapid sequence, Marcelino dos Santos, FRELIMO's sec-

ond-in-command, and then Sebastião Marcos Mabote, deputy defense minister and chief of the Mozambican general
staff, traveled to Moscow. In the first week of June, their
visits were reciprocated by the arrival in Maputo of a high-
ranking Soviet military delegation, led by the head of the
main political directorate of the Soviet army and navy. This
delegation stated in very general terms Soviet willingness
to intensify military cooperation, but does not seem to have
been very forthcoming in terms of promising a substantial
increase in military assistance. Soviet arms deliveries do
not appear to have increased significantly after this visit;
indeed, their dollar value in 1982 and 1983 was less than in
1978, when Soviet deliveries reached their peak. The delegation reportedly expressed in strong terms Soviet displea-
sure over the April 1982 military cooperation agreement
with Portugal, but the significance of this demarche is
questionable since nothing substantial has so far come out
of the Portugal agreement. Indeed, one may well wonder if
it might have been concluded by Machel merely to push the
Soviets toward more active military support.

In November 1982, Machel attended Leonid Brezhnev's
funeral in Moscow. Machel and Mabote had at least one
meeting with the Soviet defense minister and other leading
Soviet military officials. The concrete results of these talks
were not published. Only a few weeks later, however, South
African Foreign Affairs Minister Roelof ("Pik") Botha felt
compelled to issue a public warning to President Fidel Castro not to send Cuban troops to Mozambique, and U.S.
Deputy Assistant Secretary of State for African Affairs
Frank Wisner, who was in Maputo the same month, advised
Machel not to internationalize the war. South African and
U.S. intelligence apparently had come to the conclusion
that the Soviet and Cuban governments were considering
strengthening Mozambique's defenses.

No additional Cuban advisors or combat troops
showed up in Mozambique. Instead, Machel paid another
visit to Moscow from February 28 to March 5, 1983. This
time he was accompanied by Foreign Affairs Minister

Joaquim Chissano instead of Mabote. They met with Yuri Andropov, Foreign Minister Andrei Gromyko, and Defense Minister Dmitri Ustinov to inform the Soviet side about FRELIMO's preparations for its Fourth Congress and probably (although this was not made public) Mozambique's decision to seek an accommodation with South Africa given Maputo's lack of a military option. About two weeks later, Machel for the first time publicly acknowledged the existence of ongoing talks with South Africa seeking such an accommodation.

There is little official information available on why the Soviets and Mozambicans failed to agree on a level of military cooperation that might have saved them both from the embarrassment of Nkomati. The reluctance shown by the Soviets tends to confirm the view of many Western analysts that southern Africa is of only secondary concern to the Kremlin. And, in contrast to Angola, Mozambique lacked the hard currency to pay for modern and effective Soviet weapons. Moreover, the risk of a direct confrontation between Eastern bloc advisors and South African combat troops was much higher than in Angola. South Africa's threat to invade Mozambique in the event that Cuban troops were deployed there had to be taken seriously.

Mozambique had reasons of its own for not pushing the case for more Soviet military participation. Strong misgivings had developed about the suitability and effectiveness of the Soviet military assistance that had already been provided. As Allen Isaacman observed in the January-February 1985 issue of *Africa Report*, "Soviet weapons—with the exception of a handful of MIG-21s, MI-24 helicopter gunships, and SAM 7s—were out-of-date and costly, a fact not lost on the Mozambicans. Moreover, there was growing dissatisfaction with the quality of the conventional military training provided by Eastern bloc advisors, which proved ineffectual against the MNR guerrillas." Therefore Machel probably saw little reason to make far-reaching concessions to the Soviets on basing rights, the only way in which he might have motivated the Soviet leadership to transfer more weapons and advisors into Mozambique under acceptable terms of payment.

Some Unanswered Questions

To what extent is the legitimacy of the Soviet regime based on the pursuit of expansionist ideological goals? Is this dogma so deeply embedded in the Soviet system that it excludes any meaningful learning experiences concerning the limits of feasible ideological expansion? Western Sovietologists do not agree in their answers to this question, and on the Soviet side too there seems to be considerable controversy about this point.

On the one hand, an increasing number of Soviet economists are responding to such inescapable realities as the rising importance of East-West trade and the disappointingly modest nature of CMEA participation in Third World commerce by questioning the traditional dictum that a socialist policy should above all seek the destruction of the existing, essentially capitalist, world economic order. Today, some Soviet academics talk of a "dialectic unity of opposites" and take the position that, despite all the differences and contradictions of the two world markets, there is definite mutual interaction deriving from a number of common regularities and common tendencies that operate in the world economy as a whole.

The failure of collective agriculture in Africa has also resulted in some adjustments in Soviet thinking. As A. P. Butenko, a departmental head in the Institute for the Economy of the Socialist World System, wrote in 1982: "Neither the collective organization of labor nor the application of technology — unavoidably very simple due to limited capacities — can compensate for a loss of interest on the part of the majority of producers. . . . A reliable way of vitalizing the agricultural sector, and the economy as a whole, . . . consists in a policy which attributes top priority to the personal factors of production in this phase, i.e. in stimulating the individual work of the peasant and, by virtue of its close connection, that of the craftsman and the merchant." It is also noteworthy that a recent article by Lyudmila Alexandrovskaya and Vladimir Vigand in *Asia and Africa Today* did not once mention the Soviet Union or the other CMEA countries when asking "where do Africans place their hopes in this decade?"

But others (for example, N. Kapchenko, deputy editor in chief of *International Affairs*) still consider ideology to be of paramount importance. According to Kapchenko, "the growing scale and intensity of the ideological battle in the international arena make it imperative to step up the efforts of the socialist countries and all revolutionary forces of modern times in exposing and checking the political and ideological subversion of imperialism. . . . " Kapchenko argues from the standpoint of an ideological generalist—or "globalist" as one would say in Western terminology—rather than from that of a Third World specialist.

And there are, of course, strong tendencies in the Soviet Union, especially in the military, not to give up positions easily, because the credibility of Moscow as a superpower is seen as being at stake. This aspect of Soviet policy in the Third World is more salient in the context of relations with Ethiopia and Angola than it is in connection with Mozambique. But there is little doubt that, by and large, Soviet relations with Ethiopia and Angola suffer from the same deep structural weaknesses that have led to Mozambique's rapprochement with the West.

The Soviet system is not about to abandon its dogma of world revolutionary expansion of Marxism-Leninism, but the extent to which that goal is being put into question as a realistic option by Soviet specialists on the Third World is remarkable. By referring to Lenin's New Economic Policy (which from 1921 to 1928 permitted the existence of a limited capitalist system in the Soviet Union) as a model for today's problem-ridden socialist-oriented countries, Soviet ideologues have found a way to discuss openly and frankly all kinds of fundamental problems that Marxism-Leninism has run into, and not only in developing countries.

8

Mozambique After Machel
Gillian Gunn

December 1986

In a transition marked by solemnity but not despair, the leaders of Mozambique's governing party who survived the October 19, 1986 plane crash that took the lives of President Samora Machel and 33 others quietly agreed that Minister of Foreign Affairs Joaquim Chissano should be the successor head of state. President Chissano faces a grim challenge.

Although "approaching collapse" is a relative – and overused – term in Africa, it is an objective fact that Mozambique is approaching mass starvation and financial bankruptcy; that the country's military (Forças Populares de Libertação de Moçambique [FPLM]) is in danger of losing control of several central provinces and vital regional transport routes to antigovernment guerrillas of the MNR; and that rhetorical, economic, and military pressures by its powerful neighbor, South Africa, are increasing.

The Succession

The relatively uncontentious manner in which the succession question was resolved will help President Chissano come to terms with some of the challenges. Six days after

Machel's funeral on October 28, when his memory was honored by delegations from over 80 nations, including 18 African heads of state, the 130-member Central Committee of the country's ruling party, FRELIMO, met to decide the matter.

Although Chissano's selection was virtually a foregone conclusion, the intense if short-lived speculation in the Western press about "a succession struggle" warrants an assessment of the major "rivals."

One widely cited "competitor" was former Minister of the Interior Armando Guebuza, who is conventionally viewed as pro-Soviet and antiwhite, with solid support among the military. The reality is somewhat more complicated. Guebuza is certainly regarded as an ally by those FRELIMO members who resent the fact that whites and *mestiços* hold 16 percent of government posts although comprising only 2 percent of the country's population. Many of FRELIMO's black members are unconvinced by the explanation that a temporary imbalance is inevitable given Portugal's colonial policy of blocking black access to education. Guebuza's critics within FRELIMO concede, however, that he does not stir up this disgruntled constituency, but simply refrains from rejecting its support.

Guebuza also has a reputation for intense zeal in carrying out orders. This focus on efficiency, though much needed in FRELIMO, provokes jealousy among colleagues who fear that he will "show up" their lesser performance. His enthusiasm also gets him into trouble, as in 1984 when he implemented in a heavy-handed manner a program to move the unemployed of Maputo to the countryside. The fallout from this episode, combined with his public criticism of the March 1984 nonaggression pact with South Africa (the Nkomati Accord), led Machel to remove him as minister of the interior and temporarily have him placed under house arrest.

When things cooled down, Guebuza was given a lesser post as minister in the President's Office, and in March 1986 shifted back toward center stage, with responsibility for agriculture, light and food industry, internal trade, and tourism added to his Political Bureau tasks.

Regarding Guebuza's alleged Soviet links, the verdict is still not in. He certainly was not vocal in support of Machel's overtures to the West or the introduction in 1983 of market-oriented economic policies. On the other hand, some FRELIMO sources do not dismiss the possibility that Mozambique under a Guebuza presidency might have lurched dramatically toward the West. If he determined that such a move served the nation's interest, it is said, he would follow his past management style and execute the policy in a flamboyant and single-minded manner.

Another presidential "candidate" mentioned in the international press was Alberto Chipande, who served as minister of defense until 1983 when, while still nominally retaining his ministerial duties, he was moved to the governorship of Cabo Delgado province. The conventional wisdom is that Chipande was "demoted" because of the poor performance of the FPLM. The move to Cabo Delgado may also have been motivated by a desire to have an experienced military man overseeing developments in a key province under growing MNR pressure, and by the 1983 Fourth Party Congress decision to ensure that Central Committee members receive exposure to conditions in the rural areas. In any case, Chipande was brought back as full-time minister of defense in March 1986, and reportedly has a good relationship with both Chissano and with the military rank and file.

A third name mooted as a Chissano "rival" was Marcelino dos Santos, who held the number two position in the party hierarchy at the time of Machel's death, one rung above Chissano. Dos Santos is reputedly committed to classical Marxist ideology, and was clearly uneasy with both Machel's pragmatism on foreign policy and the late president's increasing inclination to mix market-based and conventional socialist economic policies. On the positive side, dos Santos is respected for his care not to air disagreements publicly, and for his role in the independence struggle. A key factor operating against the likelihood of a dos Santos presidency was his ethnicity. Dos Santos is a light-skinned *mestiço*, and it would be highly unlikely that FRELIMO's advocacy and practice of multiracialism could be extended to designation of a nonblack as head of state.

Who is Chissano?

Joaquim Chissano, age 47, brings to the presidency 11 years of experience as Mozambique's foreign minister and 24 years as a leading figure in FRELIMO. He is conventionally identified as "pro-Western," and South African radio has described Chissano's appointment as heralding "a somewhat more hopeful outlook for Mozambique itself and for stability in southern Africa."

Chissano was closely associated with Machel's policies and performed as FRELIMO's behind-the-scenes conciliator. He was a key actor in pulling the party through a series of factional crises in the late 1960s, and in uniting it behind Machel after the assassination of the party's founder, Eduardo Mondlane, in 1969. While holding the position of prime minister in the 1974–1975 transitional government, according to Portuguese sources, Chissano suggested that FRELIMO pursue a modus vivendi with South Africa rather than confrontation. Contrary to the conventional wisdom, Chissano did not oppose Machel's decision to sign the Nkomati Accord. Although Chissano was characterized as disapproving of the negotiations at the time, reliable FRELIMO sources identify him as one of the originators of the Nkomati idea, and say that the party decided he should maintain public distance from the accord to protect his image should the deal backfire. Chissano also shared Machel's views, stated repeatedly in the weeks before his death, that "Mozambique does not have the capacity to impose sanctions on South Africa." And, like Machel, Chissano quietly urged Angola's ruling MPLA party at least to consider the possibility of negotiations with UNITA.

Chissano was also in step with Machel on economic policy. He supported the decisions of the 1983 Fourth Party Congress to increase material incentives for peasants and loosen central control of the economy. In 1986, he called for legalization of private transport and of the purchase by tenants of their state-owned dwellings.

The positions described above do not, however, mean that Chissano is "pro-West." When I asked Chissano for his views on Mozambique's international alliances during an October 1984 interview, he took up his pencil and drew three circles on a piece of paper. Then he explained: "This is Mozambique. This is the West. And this is the East. At the moment the Mozambican and Western circles overlap considerably. But this is not necessarily a permanent state of affairs. Mozambican interests are not intrinsically overlapping with those of any other country."

Asked about official FRELIMO statements that the socialist countries are Mozambique's natural allies, Chissano responded: "The socialist countries are natural economic and political allies of the Third World, but they are not natural military allies." He defined nonalignment as involving nonadherence to any military bloc, but said that it did "not imply neutrality or equidistance between the two blocs on economic and political issues."

Chissano's public statements since he took up his presidential responsibilities suggest that he has not changed his position. The word order in his recent remark that Mozambique is "a sovereign, African, nonaligned, and socialist state" seems to be a genuine reflection of the new head of state's worldview. Regarding Mozambique's immediate foreign policy aims, his speeches have emphasized the need to improve relations with Malawi (through which FRELIMO believes South Africa is aiding the MNR), Mozambique's commitment to the Southern African Development Coordination Conference (SADCC), its fidelity to the Organization of African Unity, its support for the UN Charter, its friendship with the socialist countries, and its desire to develop cooperation with Western countries, in that order. He says that he ".... will continue ... to implement the spirit and letter of the terms contained in the Nkomati Accord rigorously."

President Chissano has also restated his endorsement of a mixed economy for Mozambique: "We want the private sector to play a useful role economically and socially, and contribute to the development of our country. To the private investor we will guarantee the protection of his property, returns on invested capital, and adequate conditions for his activities. . . . We must rigorously follow a salary policy which will reward and encourage competent workers."

Yet any expectation that Chissano will lead the country down a purely capitalist course is almost certainly unfounded. Since he became president, he has reaffirmed that "Our country has defined the construction of socialism as the objective of Mozambican society. . . . [O]nly a socialist society guarantees to the people as a whole equal rights and opportunities. . . . "

Similarly, forecasts that Chissano's preference for negotiation over confrontation may be an indicator that he will be more prepared than Machel to reach a political accommodation with the MNR seem highly speculative. In a speech immediately after taking office, Chissano warned: "The continuation of the struggle, without pause, against armed banditry in our country constitutes the most sacred and fundamental of the tasks in this phase of our history. It is a struggle in which there can be no form of compromise." Reports that he had met with anti-FRELIMO elements in New York just before Machel's death, and was going to travel to South Africa to pursue negotiations with the MNR, are dismissed by FRELIMO sources as groundless.

The Economic Inheritance

Chissano definitely will need the goodwill generated within FRELIMO by the smoothness of his succession and his past reputation as a conciliator, as well as the management skills he honed as foreign minister, to cope with the economic crises he inherited. Recent statistics make chilling reading. From 1982 to 1985, the gross domestic product declined by one-third; industrial and agricultural production went down by approximately one-half; and state expenditure increased by one-third. As of 1986, defense spending accounts for 42 percent of total expenditure (up one-tenth over 1985), the budget deficit has risen to $250 million, and foreign exchange earnings have fallen to $180 million. Mozambique's total debt is now $3 billion, and its debt service ratio has hit the incredible figure of 170 percent. This means that even if Mozambique spent all of its 1986 foreign exchange earnings on debt service, it still would not meet its debt service obligations for the year.

According to a September 24, 1986 statement by the official news agency AIM, hunger now threatens one-third of the population, and the number at risk as of September 1986 was double the figure for six months earlier. The government estimates that it will be able to provide just over one-third of the 715,000 tons of food grain that will be needed over the next 12 months, leaving a gap of about 465,500 tons of maize, wheat, and rice to be filled.

Furthermore, much economic activity now operates outside government control, and a dollar now buys 30 times as many local meticais on the black market (*candonga*) as it does at the official bank (where the rate is roughly $1=40 meticais). A factory worker's monthly salary buys him, for example, just three kilos of *candonga* apples.

Mozambique got into this economic mess through a combination of inappropriate economic policies, natural disasters, and the impact of MNR guerrilla activities over the past half-decade. Immediately after independence from Portugal in 1975, FRELIMO began to implement conventional socialist policies. Priority was placed on collectivized state farms, and help to peasant producers was focused on those who joined the largely unpopular "cooperatives."

The state farms were a disaster from the start. Although receiving the lion's share of state investment, as of

1982 they only accounted for 20 percent of total agricultural production. Shortages of management skills, inappropriate imported equipment, and the peasants' distaste for collectivized working conditions all contributed to the failure. Cooperatives worked little better, providing under 1 percent of production as of 1982.

Although the "family" sector produced over three-quarters of total output, its production also fell precipitously. Deterioration of the family sector was partly caused by the disintegration of the rural distribution network, destroyed when Portuguese petty traders pulled out abruptly at independence. FRELIMO attempted to replace the old network with state-run "People's Shops." But provision of consumer goods to stock these shops took second place behind imports of capital equipment for the state farms, and the shelves were soon bare. In the 1980–1982 period alone, the supply of consumer goods to peasants fell by a quarter.

Peasants increasingly refused to sell to the state as they realized that they would find little to buy with the meticais received in payment. Many of those who did produce a surplus gravitated toward the black market, where they received inflated prices, and used the profits to buy the few, astronomically expensive, consumer goods available in that same market. By 1982 an estimated one-half of total peasant production was being diverted through the "parallel" markets.

The industrial sector also suffered from poor planning. The state nationalized a large number of industries after independence, and private sector control of industry declined from 85 percent in 1977 to 27 percent in 1982. Although some plants were taken over for ideological reasons, FRELIMO says that many were put under state control because their Portuguese owners had fled the country and workers faced unemployment if management were not provided by the government. But the state-appointed managers were inexperienced, and a shortage of foreign exchange related to the agricultural problems made it difficult to obtain needed spare parts and raw materials. By the fourth year after independence, according to the United Nations, only 40 percent of installed industrial capacity was being used.

Much of the agricultural and industrial activity that survived government deficiencies fell victim to the escalating war in the countryside. FRELIMO maintains that South African "destabilization" – both directly through military incursions and indirectly through aid to the MNR and manipulation of economic ties – has cost Mozambique $5 billion since independence. On October 8, 1986, for example, Pretoria claimed that it had reason to believe that the African National Congress was still being allowed to operate from Mozambique, and announced that it was retaliating by ending further recruitment of Mozambican workers and expelling those already in the Republic as their contracts and work permits expired. According to J. Fourie, director of labor relations in South Africa's Department of Manpower, some 30,000 Mozambicans were employed in the South African agricultural sector in 1986, some 66,000 were employed in the mines, and an estimated 170,000 were employed illegal immigrants. If the South African action is carried out, it could cost Mozambique an estimated $50 million a year in foreign exchange earnings (about one-third of the current total).

Meanwhile, the MNR has intermittently blown up the pylons supporting the power line connecting the Cabora Bassa dam complex to South African electricity customers, and the line has been out of action for the last year. MNR disruption of railroad lines connecting hinterland countries with the Mozambican ports of Nacala, Beira, and Maputo has severely reduced income from transport service payments, which traditionally account for between one-third and one-half of the nation's foreign exchange earnings. As a result of South Africa's 84 percent reduction of cargo shipments through Maputo port since independence, and guerrilla sabotage, Maputo handled in 1985 under one-sixth of the tonnage it processed a decade earlier. Disruption of railroad lines further complicates internal economic activity, resulting in crops rotting in rural warehouses while consumer goods gather dust in portside storage facilities.

The frequency of MNR attacks on rural settlements has caused peasants in much of the country to hesitate to cultivate their fields, for fear of being kidnapped or killed. And consumer goods that do reach rural shops are often seized by the MNR. By 1983, an estimated 1,000 rural shops had been destroyed, and in that year about a quarter of the normally marketed grain was lost to the guerrillas. Though statistics are not available for subsequent years, it is safe to assume that increased MNR activities in 1985 and 1986 led to even greater disruption.

Natural disasters have also played a role in Mozambique's economic decline. The nation has historically been plagued with uneven rainfall, and headlines switch from "Starvation Due to Flood" to "Starvation Due to Drought" with depressing regularity. Portugal's neglect of the rural infrastructure during the colonial era, and the resultant lack of dams and basic irrigation facilities, have left Mozambique more vulnerable to climatic fluctuations than its neighbors. An exceptionally severe drought occurred from 1981 to 1984, leading to the 1983–1984 famine in which at least 100,000 people died and an additional 4.5 million were at risk.

Machel made some valiant attempts to rectify FRELIMO's economic policies before his death. At the Fourth Party Congress in 1983, priority was placed on small-scale projects; plans were made to break up state farms into more manageable units and encourage private sector farming; the need to decentralize planning was stressed; private industry was deemed worthy of state support; private shops were declared necessary; and the party undertook to sell off some specified industries to private entrepreneurs.

By 1986, however, many of the Fourth Congress resolutions remained unfulfilled. Because of the intensifying guerrilla war, many outlying factories and farms were inaccessible by ground transport. Consumer goods could not be delivered to the private peasant, nor spare parts to the privatized factory. Moreover, party cadres retained a bias in favor of the urban sector, not surprising since that is where most of the cadres were located. For example, the 1983 Congress called for the family agricultural sector to increase production by one-half over the following two years, while only undertaking to increase the supply of consumer goods to that sector by one-fourth. Priority access to consumer goods was to be preserved for urban workers. The chronic shortage of management skills also continued to hamper efforts to rationalize the economic structure.

The Congress did have some positive effects, however. The liberalization of economic controls, combined with the March 1984 Nkomati Accord, encouraged many Western countries to reevaluate their policies toward Mozambique, and aid began to increase, though not as fast as the government had anticipated. Mozambique joined the International Monetary Fund and the World Bank in 1984, and in 1985 obtained approval of a $45 million credit from the International Development Association, the World Bank's affiliate for concessionary lending, in support of a five-year economic revitalization program. U.S. aid increased from $4.884 million in 1983 to a peak of $66.785 million in 1985, though falling to an estimated $46.043 million in 1986. Negotiations for IMF support began, and Mozambique's decision to join the European Economic Community's Lomé Convention, the vehicle through which the EEC channels aid to the Third World, made it eligible for $135 million in aid from this source over five years.

FRELIMO's increasingly positive attitude toward foreign private investment also bore fruit. In 1986, the British firm Lonrho invested $40 million in agriculture and the U.S. company Edlow Resources Limited signed an agreement to start titanium mining. In general, however, foreign companies hesitated to invest because of the insecure transport system.

In sum, though the war has been only a partial cause of Mozambique's economic problems, and FRELIMO's policy mistakes have played an important role in the economic decline, the war is an effective barrier against economic recovery. Even if policy mistakes were to be vigorously rectified, as Chissano apparently intends, recovery will be partial at best as long as the cities remain cut off from the countryside by guerrilla activity and the transport networks serving the hinterland countries continue to be sabotaged.

The Military Inheritance

Mozambique's already bleak military situation underwent a further sharp deterioration just before Machel's death. In September 1986, well before the start of the rainy season which usually marks an increase in guerrilla activity, the MNR began a new offensive.

The timing seems to have been affected by a September 11 confrontation between the leaders of Mozambique, Zimbabwe, and Zambia on the one hand and Malawi's President H. Kamuzu Banda on the other. The three charged that the MNR had been allowed to establish bases in Malawi, and demanded that Banda dismantle these bases and turn the MNR guerrillas in his country over to Mozambique. Banda apparently responded by simply telling the MNR to leave the country, and on September 17 the exodus began, with a reported 10,000 guerrillas crossing into Mozambique. For the first time in its history, the MNR actually took control of border towns and held them. By mid-October it controlled Mutarara in Tete province, Caia in northern Sofala, and Milange in Zambezia province. Ironically, Mozambican peasants fled from the new war area into Malawi to escape MNR actions, and by the end of October UN officials reported that 40,000 had taken refuge in the neighboring state.

Even more worrying for FRELIMO, the MNR took the strategic bridge across the Zambezi river, which links the north and south of Mozambique. Control of the bridge also permits the MNR to infiltrate further into Sofala and Zambezia provinces. If it establishes a presence all the way to a province's coast, it will have effectively cut a swath through the center of the country. Diplomatic sources suggest that the MNR's objective is to divide the country so that it can set up a rival government in the north and appeal for international recognition.

Military tensions between Mozambique and South Africa also escalated in the weeks preceding Machel's death. On October 6, a land mine exploded in the Transvaal not far from the Mozambique border, injuring six South African Defense Force (SADF) personnel. The next day Minister of Defense (General) Magnus Malan accused Machel of permitting the African National Congress to infiltrate through Mozambican territory to plant the mine, and warned: "If President Machel chooses terrorism and revolution, he will clash head-on with South Africa." This was swiftly followed by the previously mentioned announcement of a cutoff of labor recruitment from Mozambique.

FRELIMO countercharged that South Africa had infiltrated a commando unit into Mozambique, that "over the last few weeks, South Africa [had] organized the massive introduction of armed bandits into Tete and Zambezia provinces from Malawian territory," and that "high ranking civilian and military circles of the Pretoria regime are personally guiding" these "bandits." Malan retorted: "When the ANC commits terror against South Africa from neighboring countries, the leaders of those countries are co-responsible." In turn, Mozambique's state news agency AIM announced just two days before Machel's death that it had received private warnings of a plot being hatched by some elements in the South African military to assassinate Machel.

The crash of Machel's plane in South African territory added to the tensions between Pretoria and Maputo. Many in FRELIMO considered it entirely possible that elements in the South African military had orchestrated the assassination of the Mozambican leader. To date, however, the official Mozambican position has remained that Machel died "in circumstances that are still unclear."

The abrupt decline in the government's military situation and the escalation of tensions with South Africa just before Machel's death were the culmination of a long process. The story began in 1976, when Rhodesia's intelligence service set up the MNR, recruiting a mixture of disgruntled whites, FRELIMO dissidents, and others. The main purposes of the MNR at this time were to punish FRELIMO for aiding Robert Mugabe's Zimbabwe African National Union (ZANU) guerrillas, who were fighting for majority rule from bases in Mozambique, and to gain intelligence on ZANU plans. The organization's military activities initially were merely disruptive, and the MNR did not seek to engage the FPLM during its first few years of existence.

Ironically, the MNR's transmutation into a genuine threat was the result of the disappearance of its initial patron. According to sources close to the MNR, a few days before the scheduled hand-over of power to an independent black government in Zimbabwe in April 1980 South African aircraft flew key MNR personnel and equipment to the northern Transvaal, near the Mozambique border. In 1981, these sources say, MNR guerrillas were transported back into Mozambique via helicopter, and supplied by South African air drops and sea maneuvers. The MNR established a series of camps covering a wide area of the country, and, supported by its new patron, started hacking away at the nation's infrastructure.

When Machel signed the Nkomati Accord in 1984, he hoped that South Africa's undertaking to cut off its support of the MNR would convert an uncontrollable security situation into a relatively straightforward mopping-up operation. But according to documents discovered in August 1985 following the capture of the MNR's headquarters camp in Mozambique's Gorongosa game reserve, elements of the South African military violated the accord by continuing to assist the MNR.

Although the MNR, with some level of South African support, is largely responsible for Mozambique's security problems, FRELIMO's own policy mistakes have also contributed to the deteriorating military situation. Party sources readily admit that FRELIMO's failure to give sufficient attention to peasant needs, and the resultant food shortages, resulted in an apathetic peasant population, which, while not necessarily supporting the MNR, is not enthusiastic enough about FRELIMO to risk MNR retribution (reliably reported to include severing of ears, tongues, and breasts) by providing the army with intelligence on guerrilla movements. The FPLM has also been poorly trained and supplied. Stories of soldiers fainting from hunger and raiding towns for food are so common that they must contain a grain of truth. In July 1986 Minister of Defense Chipande reported that the army was short of uniforms, boots, combat rations, fuel and lubricants, communications equipment, spare parts, engineers, and doctors.

In the wake of the reformist 1983 Party Congress, Machel tried to improve the security situation by placing top priority on providing food and consumer products to the peasant populations under threat from the MNR, hoping this would win their "hearts and minds" and lead to better intelligence flows. But even when the products could get through MNR ambushes, they were seldom enough to make a difference. And in some provinces the FPLM diverted supplies for its own use.

Machel also attempted to address the problem by sending officers for training by a British mission in Zimbabwe. Since February 1986, approximately 150 Mozambicans have graduated from the 12-week British programs and returned to duty. These newly trained officers improved discipline and performance within the FPLM's top ranks, but had little effect at the lower levels, where the army interacts with the populace. In addition, even the best-trained officer will not perform well if neither he nor his men are receiving food, fuel, or ammunition.

Machel also hoped to reverse the military decline by getting better weapons. The Soviet Union has been the country's main arms supplier since independence, replacing China, which was FRELIMO's primary arms source during

the war against Portuguese colonial rule. Article Four of
the Treaty of Friendship and Cooperation concluded by the
Soviet Union and Mozambique in March 1977 states: "In
the interests of reinforcing the defense potentials of the
High Contracting Parties, they will continue developing cooperation in the military sphere on the basis of appropriate
agreements." Similar clauses about military cooperation appear in Mozambique's treaties with other Eastern bloc
countries.

In practice, Soviet military support has been less than
satisfactory in Maputo's eyes. About two weeks after a
1981 attack by South African commandos on alleged ANC
buildings in a suburb of Maputo, one cruiser and three
smaller units of the Soviet Indian Ocean fleet visited Maputo and Beira in what the Soviet ambassador called a demonstration of solidarity against further South African attacks, but little else was done in response to the raid.
Despite repeated pleas during 1982–1983 by FRELIMO
delegations to Moscow for increased military assistance
to deal with the depredations of the MNR, the dollar value
of Soviet arms deliveries in those years was less than in
1978.

Why did Mozambique and the Soviet Union fail to
strike a military cooperation bargain that might have reduced the pressure on Machel to sign the Nkomati Accord?
Some of the possible explanations are that the placement of
southern Africa in the Kremlin's current geostrategic priorities is well below other areas of the world; that Mozambique
(unlike Angola) was not in a position to pay for effective
arms with hard currency; and that the risk of a direct clash
between Soviet bloc personnel and the South African military was much higher than in Angola. Moreover, despite its
growing desperation, FRELIMO was developing some
strong misgivings over the quality of training (ill-suited for
antiguerrilla warfare) and the costly, outdated weapons offered by the Soviet Union and its allies. Under these circumstances, FRELIMO was not willing to modify its
staunchly nationalist stand against foreign military bases

on Mozambican soil as a quid pro quo for stepped-up Soviet help.

Machel also made repeated appeals to the West for arms during the 1980s, but met with little response. Britain supplied some advanced infantry rifles and the training in Zimbabwe mentioned earlier, but Mozambique's inability to pay, combined with concern about the hands into which the arms might fall, caused Britain as well as most other Western governments to balk at supplying more sophisticated weapons.

One appeal that did produce a significant response was Machel's request at a June 1985 meeting with Prime Minister Mugabe that Zimbabwe supply troops to help protect the "Beira Corridor" – a road, rail, and oil pipeline transport route that runs 170 miles from the Zimbabwean border town of Mutare to the Mozambican port of Beira. Partly because he feels indebted to Machel for the support given to ZANU's guerrilla army during the Rhodesian war, and partly because the Beira Corridor is Zimbabwe's main alternative transport route to the lines through South Africa, Mugabe agreed to help.

By mid-1986, Zimbabwe had seconded approximately 6,000 officers and men to duty in Mozambique. Although the Zimbabwean forces repeatedly ousted the MNR from its strongholds, the FPLM proved unable to hold the territory once it was placed under Mozambican responsibility. This led to the MNR and the Mozambican-Zimbabwean forces chasing each other, with neither side able to hold territory against attack by the other.

Chissano's Policy Options

Option 1. Do a Deal with South Africa. The arguments for this option are exactly those which prompted Machel to sign the Nkomati Accord with Pretoria in 1984. South African interference and/or direct aggression have contributed significantly to Mozambique's economic and military difficulties. If Pretoria's aid to the MNR were truly cut off, FRELIMO's military task would be less daunting. Mozambique's economy and the South African business community would mutually benefit from more cross-border investment in tourism, agriculture, and small-scale industry, as well as such joint undertakings as rehabilitation of Maputo port and rebuilding of the Cabora Bassa power line.

The arguments against this option are equally, if not more, convincing. South Africa's record on its Nkomati commitments does not inspire trust. Pretoria has confirmed that the references to post-Nkomati arms shipments to the MNR in the Gorongosa documents are substantially correct (but constituted only "technical violations"). U.S. Assistant Secretary of State for African Affairs Chester Crocker, responding to questions from the press in Nairobi on November 5, 1986, took a harder line: "[I]t is our impression that a pattern of communication and support does continue" between South Africa and the MNR. Asked about alleged South African arms shipments to the guerrillas, he replied: "It is our impression that the [Accord of Nkomati has] not been fully adhered to."

Another warning signal is the increase in reports of a split between South Africa's Department of Foreign Affairs and the SADF on the issue of relations with Mozambique. In 1985, following the discovery of the Gorongosa documents, Minister of Foreign Affairs Roelof ("Pik") Botha said that he was unaware until after the fact that elements of the military had continued to supply the MNR. Indeed, one of the Gorongosa documents cited an SADF officer's reference to the foreign minister as a "traitor." If the soldier-diplomat split is genuine, President Chissano has even less of a guarantee than Machel did that the civilian authorities with whom his government negotiates will be able to keep the SADF's support of the MNR in check. The possibility that the split is a red herring must also be taken into account.

In any new negotiations, Pretoria would certainly repeat its Nkomati condition that Mozambique undertake to prevent ANC guerrillas from infiltrating into South Africa across their mutual border. Mozambique's military may not be up to the job of preventing all such infiltration, and South Africa could use unintentional violations as a pretext to break the agreement. Moreover, since South Africa contends that the ANC has no effective internal network within the Republic and that all sabotage therefore must be the result of cross-border infiltration, Mozambique could be blamed by Pretoria for any internally-launched ANC actions in Transvaal province. And if the ANC is shifting to a strategy of rural sabotage and away from hard-to-control urban operations, as some observers report, there would be more opportunities for Pretoria to accuse Maputo of breaking the pact.

Chissano must also be aware that South Africa now has two reasons for aiding the MNR, rather than the one reason it had in 1984. It still wants to pressure Mozambique not to support the ANC, but sanctions are an added priority. If, as seems increasingly evident, South Africa intends to use its neighbors as hostages in the sanctions game, there may be greater incentive to help the MNR keep regional transport routes to Africa's east coast closed, while also continuing to aid Angola's UNITA guerrillas in keeping the west coast route out of action. This two-pronged strategy could force southern Africa's six landlocked states to continue to channel some 85 percent of their trade through South African ports, and leave them vulnerable to a transportation cutoff that might be imposed by South Africa in retaliation for a push by them for sanctions.

Pretoria's willingness to use the transport weapon both as a deterrent and as a retaliation against sanctions has already been demonstrated by its August 1986 slowdown of shipments across the South Africa-Zimbabwe border just after Prime Minister Mugabe participated in a Commonwealth mini-summit at which increased sanctions were discussed. If South Africa were to cut off the MNR completely, this valuable lever would be eroded.

Finally, Chissano would probably face considerable opposition within FRELIMO to more deal-making with South

Africa. Although the official Mozambican position is that Machel died "in unclear circumstances," the angry demonstration in front of South Africa's Maputo trade office after Machel's funeral was evidence that many citizens believe Pretoria engineered the crash, perhaps by broadcasting false navigation signals to mislead Machel's pilot. Given Machel's moderating influence within the Front Line states grouping, it is not obvious what advantage Pretoria could have gained from his death, especially a death within South African territory. Logic aside, Chissano would be assuming an enormous political risk to take an Nkomati II initiative in the present highly emotive period.

Option 2. Turn East. The principal argument against this option is that the Soviet Union remains reluctant to increase its economic or military involvement in Mozambique. While Cuba's relationship with FRELIMO is qualitatively different from the Soviet Union's (for example, Western diplomats credit Castro with having mediated between Machel and the Kremlin over the signing of the Nkomati Accord), an infusion of Cuban personnel could not make a significant difference in the military situation unless Mozambique were to receive large supplies of Soviet arms.

Chissano could try to arouse Soviet interest by offering Moscow a base facility, but such an offer would violate a basic tenet of FRELIMO policy dating from its 1962 founding documents. The principle of not allowing any foreign military bases ("with no exception") was reaffirmed in the 1978 constitution. Moreover, some military experts believe that the Soviets' strategic requirements have changed so much since Mozambique's independence in 1975, when the USSR sought such rights, that a base might not be attractive to the Soviet Union now.

In addition, the West, and particularly the United States, would react extremely negatively to any increase in Soviet and Cuban involvement. Aid could be jeopardized, and there would be pressure from the right in Washington for U.S. aid to the MNR.

Option 3. Turn More to the West. Past experience suggests that, even given the political will to do so at the top level, the U.S. and European governments might not deliver the kinds and levels of support Mozambique needs. After Machel signed the Nkomati Accord, the Reagan administration wanted to provide significant aid and nonlethal military assistance. But pressure from the right in Congress and elsewhere in the policy community succeeded in limiting economic aid to that which directly assists the private sector, and in blocking all military aid.

In addition, foreign aid spending is coming under both budgetary and domestic political pressures in a number of Western donor countries, including the United States. The prospects of a sizable new aid initiative for Mozambique at a time when allocations for "proven friends" are threatened with cuts are limited. Moreover, otherwise sympathetic officials may be hard-pressed to defend investment in projects (such as the Beira Corridor transport route) that Pretoria has the power, and increasingly the will, to destroy.

Chissano also has to keep in mind the possible impact of a major turn to the West on relations with the Soviet Union and its allies. While economic links with the West have been tolerated, and there is reason to believe that Moscow would welcome further sharing of the economic and military assistance burden, an overtly anti-Soviet stance by Mozambique in international fora could result in reduced assistance from the socialist countries.

Option 4. Do a Deal with the MNR. One major problem with this strategy is the difficulty of identifying with whom such a deal might be negotiated. In 1984, for example, South African-sponsored negotiations between FRELIMO and the MNR had seemingly produced an agreement (the "Pretoria Declaration") that inter alia acknowledged Machel's authority as president and called for an end to armed conflict within the country. But the MNR's then secretary-general, Evo Fernandes, backed out of the deal within a week, possibly because of the influence of an MNR faction closely connected with Portuguese industrialists who had lost their properties to FRELIMO nationalization, and who wanted the war continued until they could be assured of the return of these properties.

The MNR's internal situation has become even more confused since the breakdown of the Pretoria Declaration. In July 1986, a new organization calling itself the Committee for Mozambican Union (CUNIMO) was founded in West Germany. A CUNIMO press release praised the MNR's leader, Afonso Dhlakama, and claimed that CUNIMO was laying "the foundation for a permanent civil administration following the end of the civil war." CUNIMO apparently envisaged itself as a "political" wing of the MNR, which has long been criticized for lacking a clear political platform. Dhlakama promptly denied that CUNIMO had any affiliation with the MNR. When CUNIMO tried to send a representative into Mozambique to meet with Dhlakama and clarify the issue, the envoy was stopped at the Malawi-Mozambique border on Dhlakama's orders.

The CUNIMO-MNR squabble reflects two underlying strains among those Mozambicans actively opposed to FRELIMO: racial/ethnic tensions and the question of under what circumstances negotiations with FRELIMO should be initiated.

A major component of the ethnicity problem is white-black tension. Black MNR members resent the privileged positions enjoyed by some whites, and particularly the high profile taken by Fernandes, a white Portuguese citizen who held the post of MNR secretary-general until July 1986. Because of the difficulties of communication with Dhlakama (who seldom sets foot outside Mozambique), Fernandes took many independent decisions and cultivated the image of de facto MNR head. He also derived considerable power from his connections with business interests in Portugal and Brazil.

A 1983 attempt spearheaded by Artur Vilankulu (who is black) to strip Fernandes of his secretary-general credentials failed, and it was Vilankulu who ended up being expelled; he is now spokesman for CUNIMO. A new black-led drive, in July 1986, succeeded; the post of secretary-general was abolished, and Fernandes was demoted to "Chief of Studies and Ideology." The move defused some black-white tension, but other whites still retain their positions and the racial strain is still evident.

The MNR also suffers from regional-tribal differences. Most of its black leaders come from the center of the country, and many are affiliated with the Manica tribe, possibly because the Rhodesians found it geographically convenient to recruit from Mozambique's central provinces when forming the organization. The MNR is trying to cultivate leaders from other parts of the country, but progress is slow. Manica domination inevitably causes some unease among the MNR's ethnically more diverse lower ranks.

The negotiations issue is possibly even more divisive. CUNIMO spokesman Vilankulu has put forward relatively flexible conditions at times, only to state later that he opposes all negotiations and supports total military victory. Depending on whom one talks to within Dhlakama's MNR, the organization is either willing to agree to anything that guarantees free elections in Mozambique, or believes it can win the current war and is only interested in a power handover. And even the same individual within the MNR may have one set of conditions for negotiations one month, and a different set the next. The latest "MNR position," announced in Washington on September 29, 1986, offers a cease-fire and amnesty to FRELIMO in return for free elections and the expulsion of foreign troops.

Since all individuals calling themselves MNR representatives agree that Dhlakama is the MNR's leader, one might think that he could clarify the negotiating conditions. But outsiders must usually rely on his representatives to convey messages, making confidential discussions virtually impossible. Furthermore, those who have met Dhlakama say he is more at home with military than with political tactics, and has not decided what his priorities would be in negotiations.

Yet another factor complicating negotiations is the diversity of the MNR's sponsors and their priorities. The movement reportedly receives or has received aid (a) from South Africans who want FRELIMO to do more to restrict the ANC, and possibly want the Front Line states to undertake not to lobby for sanctions; (b) from Portuguese and Brazilian industrialists, who want the return of nationalized properties; (c) from Middle Eastern interests seeking to pressure FRELIMO for guarantees that the Muslim population of northern Mozambique will have religious freedom; (d) from Mozambican exiles, some of whom want power returned to traditional chiefs; and (e) from American and European conservative groups opposed to all Third World governments linked in any way to the Soviet Union or Cuba. As the 1984 Pretoria Declaration incident shows, MNR conditions tend to change according to which external backer has the negotiator's ear at a given time, and so the large number of sponsors does not bode well for a settlement.

Even a deal with FRELIMO that was acceptable to all MNR factions and backers would not guarantee an end to the war. The MNR is not an army with an authoritative central command. Many of its recruits join up because that is the simplest way to survive. If a young man is on the verge of starvation, joining the MNR and thereby receiving a weapon with which to steal food is an attractive option. Even if there is an official cease-fire, the rank and file will continue to pillage as long as it is without provisions. Since food production cannot increase until peace returns, a vicious cycle is possible. Already, as occurred in Uganda, violence is becoming a way of life for significant portions of the population.

Finally, doing a deal with the MNR could cause serious problems within FRELIMO. Because so many FRELIMO members have had friends or family mutilated or killed by the MNR, there is a growing hatred for "the bandits." Any deal would presumably involve MNR members receiving some government posts. The longer the war continues, the less likely it is that Chissano could integrate MNR figures into the government structure without dividing FRELIMO.

Option 5. Escalate Pressure on Malawi. Many in FRELIMO believe that a large portion of South Africa's aid to the MNR is coming across the Malawi border.

Mozambique and its allies among the Front Line states have the means to put considerable pressure on Malawi. All Malawi surface trade must pass through Mozambique, Tanzania, or Zambia. If these states were to close their borders, all non-air traffic would stop and Malawi would be virtually paralyzed economically. On the other hand, it is not at all certain that the Malawian authorities, even with the best of intentions, could cut off all MNR crossings. Part of the Mozambique-Malawi frontier runs through Lake Malawi, which is hard to patrol, especially at night.

Recent South African actions have produced additional obstacles to a get-tough policy toward Malawi. On November 6, 1986, Foreign Minister Botha provided the press with documents he identified as having been recovered from the plane that carried Machel to his death. These documents were described as transcripts of an October 16 meeting in Maputo between Zimbabwean and Mozambican officials at which plans to topple Banda were discussed. The plot was said to involve destroying the bridges linking Tanzania and Malawi, recruiting Mozambicans living in Malawi to destabilize the regime, and organizing a "Malawi Liberation Front."

Mozambique has vigorously denied the allegations, and there is evidence that the documents were tampered with, but, real or fabricated, the documents render any Mozambican action against Malawi more risky. As President Julius Nyerere learned when Tanzania became directly involved in the overthrow of Idi Amin's regime in Uganda in 1979, Africans take seriously Article III of the Charter of the Organization of African Unity, which forbids disrespect for the sovereignty and territorial integrity of member states, subversive activities aimed against them, or interference in their internal affairs.

Option 6. Focus on Economic and Military Reform,

with Help from Zimbabwe. This option involves four major elements:

(1) Move the younger generation to the fore in the military. There has long been dissatisfaction within FRELIMO at the excessive respect paid to the *historicos*, the now-aging figures who played leading roles in the liberation struggle. Although many have proven unprepared for their postindependence tasks, Machel hesitated to demote them for the sake of unity. Instead, the *historicos* were rotated from one responsible position to another. This policy blocked a new generation of young, more technically skilled army officers and civilian administrators from moving into top posts. A major overhaul of the military (including forcing the *historicos* into retirement) would give the younger guard a chance.

(2) Move the most competent administrators from the civilian sector to the military sphere. Many of the military disasters stem from poor planning and logistics. The FPLM has already been relying on civilian administrators for advice, but under this strategy the experts would actually be integrated into the army.

(3) Implement vigorously the economic reforms outlined in the Fourth Party Congress of 1983. This would involve providing more material incentives for peasants and forcing the urban sector to accept the austerity rural rehabilitation will require.

(4) Encourage Zimbabwe to send in more troops and use them not only to take but also to hold territory. This would end the cycle of Zimbabwean soldiers taking towns only to have FRELIMO soldiers lose them.

A major advantage of this four-part strategy is that it relies primarily on national and regional resources. In addition, the only foreign state directly involved, Zimbabwe, has both a record of military competence and a major strategic interest in reestablishing peace in Mozambique. If the Mozambican transport routes were cut, Zimbabwe would be almost entirely dependent upon South Africa for surface transport. Indeed, Mozambican and Zimbabwean interests overlap in so many areas that Chissano recently speculated on the possibility of a future federation between the two countries. Mugabe told the Zimbabwean parliament in November 1986: "The survival of Mozambique is our survival. The fall of Mozambique will certainly be our fall." Zimbabwean Minister of State for Security Emmerson Munangagwa subsequently added: "It [the Beira Corridor] is so important that we will keep it open at every cost."

This option would also ease some of the racial strains in FRELIMO, much of whose older guard is nonblack. Because FRELIMO has implemented equal opportunity in education, the younger generation is more racially balanced, though nonblacks still make up a disproportionately large percentage of the skilled personnel. Moving the younger generation to leadership positions in the military would improve the relative position of blacks.

A shift of civilian administrators into the military, however, would not be cost-free. The civilian sector is already badly understaffed, and the siphoning off of management skills from the civilian to the military sphere could contribute to even greater peasant apathy, adding new complications to the military situation.

Another problem with this strategy is that a reorganization of the military aimed at increasing its competence would violate one of the basic principles underlying FRELIMO unity. Under Mondlane and Machel, individuals who "made mistakes" were not demoted. They were moved gently to one side and after a decent period reintegrated into the leadership in another role. This partly explains why FRELIMO is one of the few African parties not to suffer from major factional splits.

If Chissano moves against the *historicos*, he will face opposition from the old guard. Machel was reportedly planning such an overhaul at the time of his death and, given his hold on the affection of the FRELIMO membership, he probably could have pulled it off. But Chissano, despite his impeccable party credentials, cannot draw on the same reservoir of emotional support. Therefore, he will have to act cautiously – at a time when speed is critical if the MNR is to be prevented from slicing the country in two.

Another possible problem revolves around Minister of Defense Chipande. Machel reportedly had Chipande's support for this strategy. But with Machel no longer there to protect him, taking responsibility for implementing a sweeping military shake-up involves major political risks. Chissano may not want to subject Chipande to such dangers.

There is a final question that Chissano must face in evaluating this option: Is the Mozambican military already so demoralized that even an influx of new blood, civilian administrative skills, and additional Zimbabwean troops would be insufficient to turn the situation around?

Chissano's Likely Choices

Given the hazards associated with each of the six options, Chissano is unlikely to embrace any one of them fully. According to sources close to the Mozambican government, doing a deal with South Africa, negotiating with the MNR, and turning vigorously to the East or to the West are all ruled out for the time being.

Chissano is reportedly most inclined toward Option 6 (improving FRELIMO's own economic and military performance and getting greater Zimbabwean commitment to the war), partly because it is a logical extension of Machel's plans at the time of his death and would therefore have a better prospect of approval by the FRELIMO Central Committee. This will probably be combined with Option 5, encouraging Malawi to halt MNR aid flows, though the pressure Chissano exerts will now have to be more overt and diplomatic than covert or military. A modified version of Option 3, turning to the West, is also envisaged. And though a major new agreement with South Africa is unlikely, Chissano will seek to smooth relations with Pretoria within the framework of the existing Nkomati Accord.

Chissano confirmed many of these impressions in his first press conference as president, held on December 4, 1986. On South Africa, he insisted that Mozambique was not providing any operational aid to the ANC, and refrained from blaming Pretoria for Machel's death. He promised major economic reforms, including an austerity program that he said would be "like removing a parasite from your foot — very painful but in the end good for you." He expressed faith in Malawi's commitment to cooperate with Mozambique in a recently established joint security commission, and spoke of his hopes that Britain, France, the United States, West Germany, Spain, Italy, and Brazil would supply arms. As expected, he was adamant in his refusal to negotiate with the MNR.

Chissano's maneuvering room, however, is restricted by the stresses Option 6 could place on FRELIMO unity. He made it clear that maintaining unity is a top priority when he expressed faith in the officials appointed by Machel in a November 13, 1986 speech to the opening session of his Council of Ministers: "Their cooperation is fundamental to the success of my mission. . . . I want to appeal that this unity should be neither temporary nor superficial nor conditioned by the emotions of the moment. . . . During this difficult period, more than ever before, there is a need to close our ranks, to make our government a monolithic, cohesive, and unwavering bloc — a body impenetrable to enemy thought and action."

If Chissano's strategy fails, and the military situation continues to deteriorate, FRELIMO will not necessarily be ousted from power, but it could find itself in control only of the southern part of the country, and perhaps only in the urban areas of the south. This is not an unprecedented situation in Africa. Angola's ruling party, for example, has virtually ceded a chunk of its southern territory to South African occupation and UNITA guerrilla control. But a long-term stalemate could cause major problems for Mozambique's neighbors by keeping the central and northern transport routes inoperative and permitting intermittent sabotage of the southern ones. Such a standoff would also tip the strategic balance in southern Africa even more firmly in favor of Pretoria.

Index

147